ENNISCORTHY
History & Heritage

ENNISCORTHY
History & Heritage

Micheál Tóibín

New Island Books

Enniscorthy: History & Heritage
First published 1998 by
New Island Books
2 Brookside
Dundrum Road
Dublin 14
Ireland

British Library Cataloguing in Publication Data
A catalogue record for this book is available from the British Library

ISBN 1 874597 79 0

New Island Books receives financial assistance from The Arts
Council (An Chomhairle Ealaíon), Dublin, Ireland.

Cover photo: Bord Failte
Cover Design: Slick Fish Design, Dublin
Typesetting: New Island Books
Printed in the Republic of Ireland by Colour Books, Dublin

Contents

About the Author

Micheál Tóibín (1913-1967) was born in Enniscorthy. He studied at University College Dublin and taught for many years in the Christian Brothers School in Enniscorthy. In the early 1960s, with Fr Joseph Ransom, he founded the Wexford County Museum at Enniscorthy Castle. His articles and essays on the history of Enniscorthy appeared in many journals and periodicals.

☙

Acknowledgements

Acknowledgement is made to the editors of the *Enniscorthy Echo*, *The Past*, *An Leabharlann* and *The Cathedral Souvenir* where these articles and essays first appeared. Thanks also to Mr Bill Lett of Enniscorthy for kindly showing us the old friary door in his premises. And thanks to New Island Books — to Dermot Bolger, whose idea this was, and to Ciara Considine, who worked on the manuscript which such care and attention. Thanks for her zeal and enthusiasm.

I have left footnotes where I felt they might be useful for other researchers.

— Colm Tóibín

INTRODUCTION:
THE STONES OF ENNISCORTHY

Everywhere you notice the changes. The two roundabouts, for example. You see the first as you approach the town on the sleek new Dublin road; the other is in the Abbey Square, close to the site of the old Franciscan Friary whose tower collapsed in the Big Wind of 1839. Or the new cinema, close to the site of the old Portsmouth Arms Hotel, which was called after the Earls of Portsmouth, the Wallop family, who – granted much land in the town and the surrounding territory in the sixteenth century – made their fortune out of the forests between Enniscorthy and Mount Leinster and restored the castle and converted the friary for domestic use. Or the two new hotels; or the new apartment blocks everywhere; and all the traffic.

Some things are missing. The old Cotton Tree on the western side of the bridge has gone. The Folly river, a tiny canal, which once made its way from the Urrin river towards Lett's Brewery, running through the gardens of Cliff House, by the side of the tennis club and then parallel to John Street, is nowhere to be found. Bolger's department store on Rafter Street has become Dunnes Stores and the old system of payment – dockets and money put into a round metal container and rocketed through metal pipes to a central cash office and then change and receipt rocketed back – was dismantled more than twenty years ago. And almost all of the industry has gone. For many years Enniscorthy's rich hinterland meant that it had a thriving flour mill, a thriving maltings and a thriving bacon factory, all three of which were family owned and all three of which provided employment for all sections of the community.

The whole atmosphere of the town depended on these factories: on certain days you could hear the pigs squealing on their way into the factory. In summer, there was a permanent smell of dust and grain in the vicinity of the mill and the maltings. In the 1960s when I was growing up, both industries were expanding. Over the hump of the railway bridge the maltings added new iron lungs, the mill built new offices beside the silos. And the owners seemed posh and patrician: Old Mr Browne who owned the mill was remote and exceptionally polite, there was a kind of steely innocence about him. It seemed natural that he should own a mill. The owners of the maltings had their own mystique, they had once lived in the Castle in the middle of the town. In the 1960s the owner of the bacon factory built a huge modern house outside the town. No one had ever seen so much glass.

These people had inherited the earth − the idea that someone could own a factory that had not inherited one was not current at the time − and we had inherited our place in the world they created. We knew that this world too had come about as a result of change because all around us in the town were reminders of an earlier way of life. There were warehouses made of cut stone close to the river for the storage of grain, most of which were derelict (some are being restored as apartments); there were quays made for river transport (the coming of the railway made these redundant). In the mid-1960s my father wrote an article in *The Echo* to mark the dismantling of Lett's old millwheel. He wrote:

> "Lett's millwheel has been a leading landmark well-known to Enniscorthy's citizens for several generations. Itself a work of art, the millwheel bore the date 1849 and was the work of Murphy of Wexford. The watercourse which operated the millwheel was in existence in the eighteenth century and over several centuries has served the industrial life of Enniscorthy very well. Messrs Lett's premises were formerly an ironworks, later used as a mill and subsequently as a brewery. Before passing into the hands of the Lett families − an honoured name in the

life of Enniscorthy — it was owned by the Pounders, who before 1798 leased it to William Barker, the Insurgent leader. The passing of the old millwheel will be a source of regret to the older generation of Enniscorthy's citizens — it is the severance of an ancient link with the town's past."

But none of these signs of change really prepared anyone for the changes which were to come: at first they were small, just changes in name, the name of Mosse was added to Davis of the mill, Roche's maltings became Roche Gibney. No one thought too much about this — it was part of the general process of modernisation and consolidation. But now that these small industries have closed, or are as good as closed, the process behind the change seems to have been inevitable. They did not close because of falling profits, or shifts in the market. They closed because of take-overs, they closed because a larger conglomerate moved in seeking a larger monopoly; they closed because such small town industries are a thing of the past. They will not open again; the processing of grain, which has been the basis of the town's economic life for hundreds of years, is finished, like the river traffic and the Folly river.

The town is full of new buildings, and despite the closures, there is new energy and activity and a sense of money. Some things have improved. The Market Square has been re-designed; it has become a civic space rather than a car park. The library and the fire brigade building have been moved to the Back Road — the library used to be at the very top of the Urban District Council Offices, the fire brigade in the busy Market Square. The Cathedral, which recently celebrated its one hundred and fiftieth anniversary, has been magnificently and tactfully restored, using many of Pugin's original colours and ideas.

All around is a sense of the past. The monuments in the Market Square and the Duffry Gate to 1798, the names of the surrounding villages and towns in the songs about the rising, the view of Vinegar Hill, all make clear that this was once a market town, but it was also once a battlefield. Other reminders are there too: the medieval ruins in Templeshannon of what was once the only settlement in the town have recently been cleaned up. Street names like Rafter Street and Weafer Street remind us of figures from the War of Independence. Other names like Abbey Square, Friary Hill and Friary Place remind us of the Franciscan Friary which thrived for more than a hundred years between the banks of the Slaney and Lett's Brewery. And it is astonishing when you walk into Lett's Brewery now to find that there is an old doorway from the Friary — beautiful, glistening, cut granite, perfectly preserved — set into a modern wall. Looking at it is like entering into a Thomas Hardy novel where Wessex in the second half of the nineteenth century is haunted by an earlier world which is close by — Roman maybe or earlier still — which casts a strange, lingering shadow on the contemporary world.

And it is even more astonishing when you walk up Castle Hill and notice that the Castle has a similar doorway. This must have been put there after the Dissolution of the Monasteries, or sometime in the second half of the sixteenth century or the early seventeenth century when the Wallops were modernising the Castle and the old Friary was being used for domestic purposes and could be easily plundered and its beautiful granite doorways moved.

It is hard to think of another building with the same squat, determined shape as Enniscorthy Castle. It was built by the Normans to withstand weather and time, and strengthened by the English to remain a symbol of their dominance from the reign of Elizabeth onwards. I love the idea of it standing alone there at the top of the hill, nothing solid in sight except the ruins of Templeshannon and the Franciscan monastery at St John's; and then gradually the town gathering around it, first the Franciscan monastery at the bottom of the hill and then small holdings and cabins, and slowly, with the felling of the trees, a river trade, and a market.

It has survived. My father and Father Joseph Ransom bought the Castle in the late 1950s from the Roche family —

Dodo Roche, who was brought up in the Castle, lived in the Millpark Road — and set up the County Museum there in the early 1960s. Father Ransom was the administrator of the parish of Enniscorthy; he had lived for years in Salamanca and was involved in winding up the magnificent old Irish seminary there; he had edited a book of ballads of the Wexford coast and written about local history.

I remember the old walls in front of the castle; these were built perhaps in the nineteenth century and were torn down to make the old building more accessible now that it was a museum. I remember — I must have been just six or seven — visits to the building before the work was done for the museum. I remember serious men in coats, long adult conversations and a ban on all trick-acting. My father and Father Ransom must have understood the significance of what they were doing: they were standing in the citadel, the very centre of English power in the Slaney valley, having bought the building.

I remember discovering the dungeon, cut into the rock in the very bowels of the building; it was airless and dark, with a smell of damp and mould. Soon, they put a light down there and distempered the walls — I have vivid memories of the smell of the distemper — leaving a space for the etching which someone who was imprisoned here had made in the wall — a crudely-drawn figure with armour and a sword.

Local people began to arrive with objects for the museum — old swords, coins, photographs, memorabilia, paintings. There was to be a 1798 Room and a 1916 Room. Colum Breen drew maps of Vinegar Hill and other battlefields of 1798 and using arrows and different colours he showed how the battles were fought and which way each side went. There was a room full of old carriages, one of which had belonged to the poet Moira O'Neill, mother of the novelist Molly Keane. There were two staircases in the building: the one at the front was much older — it was made of stone — than the one at the back, which was broader and made of wood. Marion Stokes, who had been a member of Cumann na mBan during the 1916 Rising in the town, had beautiful copperplate handwriting. She wrote a description of each exhibit and often these were kept in glass cases. It was difficult not to wonder if the ghosts of the Wallops, or indeed the ghosts of other Tudor adventurers in Ireland who had associations with Enniscorthy, such as the poets Raleigh and Spenser ("Sweet Slaney run softly!"), wandered now in these rooms, reading a deeply nationalist interpretation of events in the town, looking at the exhibits, listening to the committee deliberating about the future of their castle, and wondering what the world had come to, and should they let the Queen know what state Ireland had once more fallen into.

ભ

In 1969, two years after my father died, my mother, my sisters and I went to Wexford, to White's Hotel, to the launch of a new history of the 1798 Rising called *The Year of Liberty* by Thomas Packenham. I remember that somebody was giving out free cigarettes and I stuffed my pockets with them. And I remember a man whose name I recognised, who had been an associate of my father's, standing up and telling us that the real history of 1798 had yet to be written. This new book, he was sure, was not the real history. His voice shook with angry conviction as he spoke.

In his Preface to *The Year of Liberty*, Packenham had written:

> "Today, sources are embarrassingly rich on the loyalist side — ten thousand odd documents in the Rebellion Papers from Dublin Castle; a complete run of Irish newspapers, and the confidential letters of almost all the chief protagonists ... On the rebel side, lack of sources makes it impossible to do justice to the movement. I have found fewer than a hundred revolutionary documents of 1798. For the most part I have had to do with second-hand (and sometimes second-rate) material; contemporary spy reports, mid-nineteenth century biographies, folk-songs and hearsay."

The rebels left no documents then, only songs and stories, and the victors got to write history, until we became the victors, but there were still no reliable papers written by the people on our side, no letters, only second-hand, second-rate things. And it was easy then to claim that the rebellion was made up of a few misguided intellectuals and a mob, that it began with half-formed ideas of liberty, but quickly became a sectarian blood-bath. It was easy, on the other hand, to claim that it was based entirely on the influence of the American Revolution and the French Revolution and the ideas of Tom Paine; that the peasants who fought with heart and hand did so with a pamphlet about human liberty and the road to democracy in their pocket.

The Rising in Wexford, more than any other event in Irish history, is open to interpretation: it can be explained as one thing and also explained as exactly the opposite. Idealistic or sectarian; high-minded or savage; paving the way for parliamentary democracy or paving the way for mob rule; led by priests or led by Protestant intellectuals; Scullabogue was a reprisal for what happened in New Ross or Scullabogue was a vicious sectarian murder; the rebels were illiterate or the rebels were semi-fluent in French; part of a struggle which led eventually to independence or chaotic in its origin and results; a disaster or a noble moment in Irish history.

Commemorating the Rising, then, allows the contemporary agenda to dictate the terms. In 1898, it was a rising if the dispossessed led by rebel priests to clear the British out of Ireland, part of a Fenian agenda. A hundred years later, emphasis is being placed on the fact that it was a joint venture by Protestants and Catholics, and that it took its bearing from the French Revolution. It is clear that the commemorations are being held in the shadow of agreement in Northern Ireland and European union. Perhaps that is the purpose of history: to give depth and meaning and resonance to contemporary concerns.

But something else has also changed and this has made an enormous difference to the quality of the debate about the

Rising and indeed the quality of the commemoration. An earlier generation of historians which had written about the Rising from the British perspective had little interest in how ideas of democracy or revolution might have seeped into Wexford in the 1790s. In the 1990s, however, a new generation of historians emerged who were born and brought up in Wexford and who were acutely conscious of the gap between the monuments and songs and stories of the Rising and the scholarly work in print. Thus people like Kevin Whelan, Daniel Gahan, Anna Kinsella and Tom Dunne became the central figures in the debate about the Rising and its elements. Gahan's history of the Rising, for example, concentrates more on the plight, attitudes and movements of the rebels than the British. There are moments in his book when he points out that the rebels must have realised that the Rising would fail and what the result would be, and these moments, where the reader is allowed glimpse the world from the point of view of those who fought in the Rising, are exceptionally moving and melancholy for anyone who comes from Wexford.

My father taught with the Christian Brothers whose arrival in the town he chronicled; whose move from the Island Road to the Millpark Road he noted. The Brothers lived in the monastery beside the school which they built at the end of the last century. When I went to the Christian Brothers school, it seemed to all of us, teachers and pupils, that this was a world which would not change, that Brothers might go and new ones might replace them, and there would be lay teachers too, but the schools would always be run by Brothers from the monastery.

All this has changed. It has gone the way of the cash system in Bolger's and the Folly River. The Brothers have gone; vocations have dropped, and the monastery lies idle. This happened during the time when new roads were being built between Enniscorthy and Wexford and Dublin, and a new bridge and the new roundabouts. Europe was upgrading our infrastructure. During these same years Europe began to support ideas of heritage and the possibilities of more tourism, and European money was available for new heritage projects.

But this is only the context for the 1798 Heritage Centre in the old Christian Brothers monastery in Enniscorthy, which opened in April 1998 and cost two point six million pounds. From the moment you arrive, you realise that this version of events is going to be challenging and interesting. You walk across a bridge of democracy which lists cities and dates on its various planks. Athens – 592BC; Rome – 85BC, Venice – 700AD; Florence – 1378; The Hague –1581; London – 1649; Orenburg – 1773; Prague – 1775; Philadelphia – 1776; Warsaw – 1788; Budapest – 1789; Brussels – 1790; Paris – 1793; Aarau – 1798; Wexford – 1798. You realise that all of these are revolts against tyranny or despotic rulers, thus placing Wexford in a clear tradition. Then you realise that the event being celebrated in London as part of this tradition is the rise of Cromwell. Things have indeed changed, not only have the Christian Brothers gone from the monastery and the Wallops from the Castle, but the locals have decided to include Cromwell in their pantheon of those who struggled for freedom. Cromwell might be allowed a wintry smile.

The museum is history at its most high-tech, full of videos, tapes, lights and movement. No one is singing Boolavogue; there are no statues of Father Murphy. The context is wide now, the rebellion is part of a world-wide struggle against tyranny, but local things are taken into consideration too, like the changes in land holding in County Wexford from the sixteenth century. In one room, you see a tree and hear a voice asking "What is that in your hand?" A branch. "Of what?" The Tree of Liberty. "Where did it grow?" In America. "Where did it first bloom?" In France. "Where are the seeds?" In Ireland.

Military strategy is looked at: "How could our generals," a participant is quoted as saying, "for an instant think that Vinegar Hill was a military position susceptible of defence for any time, without provisions, military stores or guns?" At the end there is a game you can play with rings, and slides of famous Irish tourist sites with swans and bridges and ancient castles. At the end too there are quotes from modern historians. This is Kevin Whelan on Myles Byrne:

"Byrne's viewpoint is clear: the rebellion was not a disjointed response to unbearable provocation, but one seriously organised by a secret society with mass support, carefully planned under responsible leadership and deriving its mandate from an overwhelming popular will."

At the end, too, it states:

"While this exhibition is an attempt to present a balanced account of 1798, it is in itself an interpretation."

In 1898, those who ran the commemoration of the Rising needed to forge links to the revolutionary past, needed to establish a line of dissent and revolt which was essentially Gaelic and Catholic, needed stirring songs and martyr priests. Now, a hundred years later something else is needed — a sense of Ireland as a part of Europe, and, perhaps more important, a sense of Wexford as a place capable of creating complex and sophisticated statements about its own past, allowing dissent and re-interpretation, open to the outside world, skilled at software and video, soft lighting and ambiguous messages. The 1798 Heritage Centre is an astonishing new addition to the stones of Enniscorthy, which my father describes in such loving detail in these pages, beginning with the monastery in Templeshannon and continuing through the centuries as the town grew and developed slowly, depending on economic change and political events, now approaching the millennium with two monuments to its own past, one in the Castle Museum, and the other in the old Christian Brothers monastery where the ghosts of 1798 stand open to interpretation.

ଓଃ

ENNISCORTHY:
HISTORY AND HERITAGE

"The town of Enniscorthy stands beside the Slaney, in the centre of Wexford county; a steep town, with street climbing above street, from the Norman Castle up to where Pugin's Cathedral overlooks the scene. It is a homely, handsome place, with spacious fairgreen and squares; convents, factories, mills, stores, fine schools, overall an air of prosperity that comes from the goodness of the surrounding land and the industry of the people; a democratic place, Irish as the quartz rock on which it stands. From the centre you look across the river meadow to another hill, famous Vinegar Hill on the east bank, crowned by an ancient windmill tower, and wider prospects are through woods to the purple folds of mountains to the three heights against the sunset, that were named of old 'The three leaps of Ossin's Hounds'. If it were in France or Italy, the world would hear of Enniscorthy's beauty; painters and etchers would depict it in a hundred aspects."

The above paragraph is an extract from an article in The Capuchin Annual by the late Aodh de Blacam. Patrick Kennedy, likewise, praised the beauty of the town. In *The Banks of the Boro* he describes the scene as he stood overlooking Spring Valley:

"I went up the bye-way by Sheil's Well, and gave a backward glance at the grey castle walls, the flat green

islands above the bridge, the rushing waters of the
river, the hilly irregular streets with the grey and red
roofs, and white walls of the house."

Writers like these have found in Enniscorthy town a
charming beauty in its irregularity and steepness, its old-
world appearance in the delightful view of the town-capped
eminence overlooking the sparkling river below.

The irregularity of Enniscorthy's streets had its origin in
the rather haphazard development of the town over the
centuries. Its rise cannot be ascribed to any one period of
history. Looking back over a thousand years, we see that it
grew gradually and gracefully without conscious planning. It
is in this that its charm lies. No one could name a single year
or period, and say that it was then that Enniscorthy was
built. In fact, its growth extended over fourteen centuries,
which we can divide into a number of clearly-defined stages
of development. The story of its streets is inseparable from
the historical background.

The Shannon is, of course, the oldest part of Enniscorthy.
The word Templeshannon is derived from the Irish Teampoll
Seanain, a place-name which brings us back to the very
origins of the town. In the sixth century St Senan, in the
course of his journeyings, came here and established his
church on the east bank of the river. Beatha Seanain, The Life
of St Senan, says:

"Undertaking his journey towards Leinster, Senan
came to a certain island situated in the territory of Ui
Ceinnsealaigh near the river Slaney which is called
Inis Coirthe, and having made a stay for some time
there contracted friendship with St Maedhog, Abbot
of Ferns."

For many centuries, a small settlement existed in the
neighbourhood near St Senan's church; there is no record of
any such settlement on the east side of the river at that time.
Centuries later, the parish of Templeshannon was in the
Barony of Ballaghkeene, while the rest of Enniscorthy was in

the Barony of Scarawalsh. St Senan died in 560. At Templeshannon, near the foot of Vinegar Hill, the ruins still stand of the medieval church dedicated to St Senan, around which grew all that existed of pre-Norman Enniscorthy.

Early in the thirteenth century, a dispute arose between John St John, first Anglo-Norman Bishop of Ferns and Gerald de Prendergast. An agreement was reached which makes specific reference to "the town of Enniscorthy of the St Senan's side", clearly indicating the relative importance of Templeshannon at that time.

The first development of Enniscorthy on the west bank of the Slaney dates from the building of the Norman Castle there in the first quarter of the thirteenth century. The founder was Philip de Prendergast, father of Gerald, though the building is often ascribed to Raymond Le Gros, and even to King John. The site chosen for the Castle was an ideal one for the double purpose of commanding the Slaney valley and forming the centre from which the Duffrey could be brought under Norman sway. The Duffrey (or Dubh-Thir) was the ancient name of the extensive wooded territory between the Slaney and Mount Leinster. The same compelling factors which made the Castle site so strategically excellent, would naturally contribute to the growth in time of an important town in the Castle's environs; at a suitable fording place on the river, at the head of tidal waters, flanked to east and west by a hinterland of rich agricultural land, at the limit of river navigation, making communication easy with the haven of Wexford; here it was natural that a town should rise, with the medieval tendency to urban development. The Norman Castle provided the nucleus of this natural growth.

A few years after the Castle was built the Norman de Prendergasts founded at St John's a Priory for Canons Regular of St Victor; the Priory was made a cell of the Abbey of St Thomas in Dublin. Norman supremacy over the district continued until the resurgence of the Kavanaghs under Art Mac Murchadha at the close of the fourteenth century. For almost two hundred years from this date the Kavanaghs reigned supreme, and Norman power was at its lowest ebb.

In 1460 Donal Reagh Kavanagh, grandson of Art, founded the Franciscan Friary. The Four Masters record the foundation under that date.

Cromwell passed through Enniscorthy on his march to Wexford in 1649. In his despatch to the Speaker of the Parliament, dated 14 October, he wrote:

> "We marched into the fields of a village called Enniscorthy, belonging to Mr Robert Wallop, where was a strong castle, very well manned and provided for by the enemy; and close under it, a very fair house belonging to the same worthy person, a monastery of Franciscan friars, the considerablest in all Ireland."

Thus there were three religious foundations associated with the town, all of them by the riverside — St Senan's Church, at Templeshannon; the Priory of St John's, about a mile to the south; and almost within a stone's throw of the Castle, the Franciscan Abbey.

None of these monastic establishments survived the ravages of Tudor conquest in the sixteenth century. After the suppression of the monasteries by Henry VIII, both places were leased to John Travers, Master of the Ordnance in 1544. Grants of the property were made in the subsequent decades to numerous personages, one of whom was Edmund Spenser, to whom Elizabeth granted the Castle and Friary, but there is no evidence that the poet ever visited the place.

Finally, the Castle, lands and Friary were granted to Sir Henry Wallop, Treasurer at War for Ireland. This man was to exercise a decisive influence on the history of Enniscorthy. A man of keen business acumen, he was at once competent and far-sighted, ruthless and unscrupulous, qualities that were not uncommon amongst those Tudor adventurers. With him, the end justified the means, and in his case, the end was his own enrichment. He contributed more than any other individual to breaking the power of the native Gaelic families. He rebuilt and restored Enniscorthy Castle, and the Tudor features noticeable in the present-day building date from this restoration. When he died in 1599, he was succeeded by his son, Henry.

In 1598, the year of the battle of the Yellow Ford, we find the Kavanaghs in open rebellion, in alliance with the O'Byrnes, and in sympathy with the chieftains of the North. In May, Wallop's forces suffered severely as a result of an engagement in the neighbourhood. One account put the slain as high as 309 men; part of the town was burned when the engagement was in progress. At that time the principal channel of communication between Enniscorthy and Wexford was by Slaney navigation. When Wallop was finding it difficult to maintain supplies for his garrison, Donal Spainneach Kavanagh tried to disrupt the river traffic. Wallop built an armed boat in order to keep the highway open. A contemporary record describes the boat:

> "Sir Henry Wallop, having care of that place, as well for his owne private as for the publicke weal, did cause a small boate to be made, which carried eight tons of victuall besides men, cloase covered over head, with fourteen men and so many muskets, and a falken in the prow, by which they passed the river in despite of the rebells and victualled the garrison of Enniscorthy."

But, meanwhile, the Wallop family had commenced to reap a rich harvest from the property. From the beginning they had realised the potentiality of amassing vast riches from the great forests that stretched away to the north and west of the town. The early maps of County Wexford indicate the extent of these woodlands. "The whole country from Enniscorthy to many miles above Ferns at this time [c. 1586] was a magnificent forest of oak." (Hore, p., 412). Even as late as the date of the Civil Survey, the area under woods in the Parish of Templeshasbo (of which Enniscorthy formed a part) was estimated as high as 7860 statute acres. From the Down Survey Maps we learn that:

> "the commodities by this parish yielded are abundance of Pipe Staffs cut out of the woods, which the inhabitants at certain set times (when they are ready cut) drive before them down the river Slane in great abundance to Enniscorthy, where they fling them on shore, and then lade vessels with them; and to transport them at Enniscorthy aforesaid, they paid a certain Tribute for their landing them."

The Wallops were given the right to exact a Toll or Customs of 1/13 part of all timber passing through Enniscorthy ("all wood, viz., pipe staves, hogshead staves, barrel staves, long boards, ships planks, beams, draught timber, block timber, rafters, small timber brought to the banks of Enniscorthy ..." (Pat. Rolls of James I, June 8, 1611). The exploitation of the woodlands by Wallop was a very important factor in the economic development of the town. From the Travels of Sir William Brereton in Ireland in 1635 we are informed that "the greatest part of all the wealthy inhabitants of this town (there cannot be many) are wood-merchants". Earlier in his Diary, Sir William describes the cutting down of the forests on the banks of the Slaney tributary, the Derry ("abundance of woods, more than many thousand acres") and refers to the cost of conveying the pipe-staves "by water to Enniscorthy, which is twelve miles, at which time there is required the aid and endeavour of a hundred men to conduct and guide them in this narrow, shallow and crooked river, which runs through this wood".

In 1613, Enniscorthy became a Corporate Town, returning two members to Parliament. A few years afterwards the greater part of North Wexford was planted by James I, and many new Manors created between the Slaney and the sea. In common with other Irish towns at this period, Enniscorthy was a centre of English influence; writing in 1617, Fr Mooney said: "Anglici hæretici totum oppidum inhabitant." (translates: "English heretics inhabit the town.")

This brings us to the second important economic factor which influenced the town's rise, that is the establishment of the extensive Ironworks at Playrefield, also called Forgelands.

The man mainly responsible for setting up this considerable Ironworks was an English adventurer named Timothy Stamp. Several titled English gentlemen combined to invest large sums in the enterprise; they purchased the lands recently granted to Colonel Phayre and other grantees under the Cromwellian Settlement. In a petition dated 1664, the proprietors stated that they had expended £30,000 upon the Ironworks. An earlier petition mentioned that the petitioners had brought over to Enniscorthy "many hundred English workmen and their families". Here again the opportunity was being utilised to use the wealth of the Wexford woodlands; and when the local landlord, Dudley Colclough, protested against the destruction of the forests, a Bill was passed in the Irish Parliament confirming the right of the proprietors to fell the trees (Irish Statutes 17-18. Chas. II). The Ironworks brought considerable traffic between Enniscorthy and the Bristol Channel Ports through Wexford Harbour. Ore and cinders were transported by ship to Wexford, then by flat boats along the Slaney to Enniscorthy Quay and by horse and cart to the Ironworks at Fairfield. Robert Leigh, referring to Enniscorthy in 1684, says: "There are now two considerable Ironworks belonging to this towne, which is the reason it is well inhabited." About the same, Thomas Dinely, in the Journal of his Visit to Ireland wrote:

"Its [Wexford] situation is upon the River Slane, navigable by flatt boats to Inish Corfey, two leagues above this Town, where are Iron Works which are supplied with Iron Stone, ye mineral from ye Forrest of Dean, and some coale. This river distributes ye iron in ye countrey when made."

The records that have survived relating to these Ironworks mention Bristol, Falmouth, Gloucester, St Ives and Liverpool amongst the centres to which the products were exported. It is clearly evident that the timber trade and the

Iron Foundries were the two dominant factors in the town's growth. Each helped incidentally to destroy the forests.

Up to the end of the Tudor era Enniscorthy was a very small town, frequently described as a hamlet or village, of little importance compared to the great medieval port of Ross or the historic Danish town of Wexford. The earliest maps show the Castle with a small number of dwellings in its immediate neighbourhood. The locality was divided into Parks, or parcels of land extending outwards from the Castle — for example Bush Park, Jordan's Park, Mill Park, Rossitter's Park. However, the wood and iron industries gave an impetus to the growth of Enniscorthy. By the end of the seventeenth century it had become a town of considerable importance and this expansion continued slowly but steadily right through to the eighteenth century — but it was a growth that took an unusual form. The town extended in four long ribbon-built arms, radiating from the older central core — Irish Street to the north, John Street to the south, Duffry Street and Duffry Gate to the west and Shannon Hill top the east. The area between the arms was covered with green fields.

The first mention I can find of Irish Street in any written document is in a Wallop rental dated 1669. The street was linked with the bridge by Mary Street, which in turn was connected with Market Street by a narrow passage called Mary's Lane. To the south of Market Street, houses had been built commencing with Back Street, now Rafter Street, continuing into Guttle Street, now John Street. This was the main road from Enniscorthy to Wexford — by St John's Bridge and the hamlet of St John's. The street which is now called Slaney Street was at one time called Barrack Lane; it dated from an early period in the town's history.

The first Bridge was built across the Slaney at Enniscorthy in 1680. At that date the Town consisted of a compact built-up area, on both sides of the new Bridge, extending specially in the sector around the Castle. The longer streets leading from this central area were only beginning to emerge. During the eighteenth century there are numerous references to fires destroying the thatched dwelling-houses; the worst of these was in 1731 when, according to a contemporary magazine, 42 houses were consumed. The local Corporation look steps to establish a Fire Service, one of the first in Irish urban centres. In 1707 the Corporation ordered that "Six large iron Crooks be made, and 12 leathron Buckitts for use in case of fire," and further, that every householder within the Liberties be obliged "to keep two Barrells of Water at his door, every day and night, on the penalty of 3/4 for each Housekeeper that shall neglect; and that there be always seven men on the watch every night; that is, six men and one housekeeper, who is to command that night the watch, and he to see that they go the rounds of the town per turns three at a time, and not to go from their said watch till it be cleere Day Light".

Travellers frequently complain about the steepness of the descent to the river, and the irregularity of the smaller streets. "Its streets have two or three plots of spaciousness," wrote one topographer, "but in general are nearly as remarkable for their narrowness, as for their irregularity and capricious crookedness, and they are for the most part edificed in such a fashion as to give the town an ancient and half-Oriental appearance". Enniscorthy was now an important centre of distribution and the local industries continued to flourish, the iron foundries, timber-works, mills and tanneries, together with the smaller crafts and trades. As the century progressed malting became the leading industry; in 1796 there were no less that 29 maltsters within the urban area. The inns date from the 18th century — The Bear Inn, Fox Inn, Black Bull Inn, and later Rudd's Inn. The records that have survived from this century give us only a rare glimpse at the lives of the great majority of the town's inhabitants, who were labouring under the unequal burden of the Penal Laws. Frequent mention is made of the ruling section; of the Catholic people, men and women of the Hidden Ireland, scarcely a record remains. Their religious needs were served in the second half of the century by two thatched chapels in the outskirts of the town.

In 1798 Enniscorthy became the storm centre of the Wexford Rising. It was the first town to be captured by Irish Arms since the Treaty of Limerick was signed, over a century before. The Rising commenced at The Harrow, on May 26; Oulart Hill was fought on the following day; and on May 28 (Whit Monday) Enniscorthy was captured after a stubborn battle at the Duffry Gate. The Insurgent forces were commanded by Fr John Murphy. Then followed the fight at the Three Rocks and the taking of Wexford. The camp at Vinegar Hill was the Insurgent headquarters throughout the campaign, and the Battle fought there on June 21 ended the last hopes of an Irish victory. Two-thirds of the buildings in Enniscorthy were destroyed in the great conflagrations that formed part of these hard-fought battles. Contemporary witnesses describe the pitiful scenes after the battle of Vinegar Hill. "The town now exhibits a melancholy picture of devastation," wrote Hay in 1803, "being mostly destroyed during the Insurrection ... A fine old castle is still in tolerable repair and the town is rebuilding very fast". A considerable number of its present-day buildings date from this period of reconstruction. It was during this period of reconstruction that Weafer Street was built; that is why it was originally called New Street.

In the years between 1800 and the Great Famine, Enniscorthy expanded rapidly. Woollen mills were founded; and for a short time a cotton factory flourished. The population of the town reached its peak in 1841; it was recorded as 7,016 and of these 1,897 lived on the Shannon side of the river. There had been a big influx of people from the surrounding rural area due principally to the clearance and mass evictions that were so common a feature of the land system at that time.

To cater for the increased population, hundreds of new houses were erected. Many new roads were laid and new streets built on the green spaces between the four great arms. When a survey was carried out in 1833 there were only two houses on the Mill Park. A new wide road was then built — Mill Park Road — leading from the Abbey ground to St

John's Bridge, meeting the old road to Wexford at the bottom
of Munster Hill.

cȢ

The Slaney provided the great mode of transport and
communication between here and the town of Wexford.
There was a fleet of cots or lighters engaged in this traffic,
most of the cotmen living in The Shannon. The extensive
river navigation consisted in the export of agricultural
produce, principally corn and butter, and the importation of
coal, timber, slates, iron, salt and various other commodities.
In order to facilitate this trade, the quays on both sides of the
river had been built in the 1830s, at a cost of £9,000. It was
proposed about that time to apply for an Act of Parliament to
construct a ship canal for vessels of 200 tons burden, from
Polldarrig to Enniscorthy Bridge. Enniscorthy was then the
centre of a flourishing corn trade. The greater part of the land
was at that time, and for half a century before, under tillage,
and it was only in the second half of the century that tillage
came to be abandoned in favour of pasture. Many of the
contemporary travellers mention the thriving corn trade
here. Some years before 1846, Inglis describes "a busy corn-
market and a large concourse of people in the streets buying
and selling". "Enniscorthy ought to be a very flourishing
town," he adds, "for the corn of the greater part of the
County of Wexford passes through the market of
Enniscorthy and is shipped there." An 1846 gazetteer gives a
similar account, remarking that "the greater part of the corn
sold in the market is sent down the river to Wexford". There
was a good trade with New Ross also by land carriage.

Another big market product there was butter, a
considerable quantity of which was produced for export in
the district. The local coopers — there were over 200 of them
in County Wexford in 1851, and even thirty years later there
were 14 of that trade in Enniscorthy — were kept busy
during the Spring and Summer making firkins for the
farming community; and then in October and November, it

must have been a fine spectacle to see the farmers' carts with firkins piled in tidy tiers on top, lined up before the butter dealers' stores, on market days. One can imagine the busy scene near the quayside in those years before the railway came, when the river was the only channel of trade; then the commercial centre of gravity tended to the river-side, where merchants' stores, salt-houses, coal-yards, lime-kilns and other evidence of commerce stood in close proximity. The remains of some of these lime-kilns can still be seen in the town, just as they survive all along the course of the Slaney from Wexford — in fact all over the county — they are relics of an era when lime counted far more in the local economy than it does in our day.

As the century advanced, the volume of river traffic tended to decline. In 1868, we notice an entry tinged with not a little pathos, when Clohamon Mills were closed; it is chronicled that the "machinery was removed to Enniscorthy for shipment," having been broken into scrap on the quayside.

The advent of the railway and the development of road transport brought the river traffic to an end.

The railway was not extended to Enniscorthy till 1863. Previous to this, the town depended upon the Horse Coaches for communication with Dublin and other centres. In 1846 the journey from Dublin, reckoned at 62 miles, took ten hours. The Mail Coach left the city at 7 in the morning, reaching Enniscorthy in the afternoon at 5.40 pm. And arriving at Wexford at 7 pm. The return mail left Wexford at 6 am, coming here at 4 minutes before 8, and reaching Dublin at 6 pm. The night coach, leaving Dublin at 7 in the evening, arrived here at 5.40 am. When the 1848 leaders journeyed here on the eve of the Rising, Smith O'Brien came on the day coach, while Dillon and Meagher followed on the night coach. The route was through Bray, Wicklow, Arklow and Ferns. Before the introduction of the Penny Post, the postage charge on a letter from here to Dublin was eight pence.

The Bianconi service, with its headquarters at Clonmel, linked up Enniscorthy with the southern counties. The fare from Waterford to Enniscorthy was 5 shillings [s.], a six-hour journey. On the Royal Mail Coach from Waterford to Wexford (5 hours) the charge was 6s. (shillings) outside and 10s. inside.

In 1859 a special coach left Wexford for Enniscorthy at 9.00 each morning. Outside fare was 1s., inside, 2s. 6d. The fare on the evening Mail Coach for the same journey was 2s. outside; 3s. inside. A local newspaper in November, 1860 has the following note — "The mail coach travelling to Dublin was an hour late on Monday night, owning to an accident occurring on the road by the breaking of the pole" — showing the punctuality that was expected from the mail coaches. On June 30, 1863, the last mail-coach left Dublin for Wexford.

Previous to the construction in the 1830s of the Island Road and Blackstoops Road, the old coach route from Dublin, through Scarawalsh, crossed up "Jack's Lacks" (the remains of the old Bridge over the stream are still there), down the Bohreen Hill, up Irish Street, into the old Barracks, across Mary Street, then unbroken by the Railway, across Templeshannon, up Shannon Hill, and continued on the old road to Wexford. Remembering this hilly route, it is little wonder if the topographer complains that the streets are "in some parts inconveniently steep for carriages".

Talk about the coach roads invariably leads to mention of the taverns and hostelries that marked their course. Rudd's Hotel at Templeshannon (later Mr J. J. Bennett's Portsmouth Arms Hotel) is mentioned as a stopping place, while various other centres are also mentioned. Taverns were plentiful in olden times — the names of a few were "Red Pat's"; the "Colleen Rua's" at St John's; another below Motabeg; the Rock Tavern on the Scarawalsh Road; and at Blackstoops, only two generations ago, there was a busy tavern, where tradition tells us that punch was sold for 2½ d. a tumbler!

A study of the old coach routes is extremely interesting and old people love to tell how the old roads went, in relation to the many "New Lines" that exist in this country, most of which were constructed in mid-nineteenth century, many of them as part of the Famine Relief Works.

It is easy to appreciate the viewpoint of the traveller, who wrote in 1846 that "Enniscorthy is so singularly irregular, that in spite of the smallness of its extent, no tolerable idea can be conveyed of its street alignment except by means of a map". The streets have seen a great deal of alteration, of demolition and reconstruction since then. Most of the old narrow alleys are gone; many new streets built; many of the green spaces of a hundred years ago have provided sites for our modern housing schemes.

Above the Cathedral, extensive rows of houses on both sides flanked a rather narrow street leading to the Duffry Gate, to the "Beaver Hats" (now the premises occupied by Mr Joseph Doyle). There were lines of houses on two sides of the present Fair Green – facing the lower Duffry Gate and Convent Road. On one side the Duffry Gate houses extended only as far as Hayes' Field, but on the right went a great deal further up. Patrick's Street is of much later origin, as is the greater part of the present Ross Road. At the lower part of the latter road, several small lanes ran left and right, each containing many small thatched dwellings. Pig Market Hill was cut off from Wafer Street (then New Street) by a block of buildings which has since disappeared, while, situated at the rear of the present Fairview Terrace (then called Spout Lane) was a small enclosure called Spout Square. Lymington Road, like the Hurstbourne Road, was not built till about 1860, their names being derived from the English title and residence of the town's absentee landlords.

The old road from the Market Square to the Urrin Bridge ran as at present through Rafter Street (then known as Back Street) through Court Street and St John Street (named Guttle Street) and down by the County Home. This was the road travelled by the loyalist refugees to Wexford in 1798. There were several narrow by-ways leading from this main road — the Hospital Lane, leading to the old Fever Hospital, and another down by the Folly to Mill Park Road. On the latter road there was only one row of dwellings, opposite Lett's

Brewery (then Pounder's Brewery and Mill); for the rest it was a mere green field stretching from the road to the river bank, flanked by some stores, malt-houses and lime-kilns. Nearer the town we find Freeman's Flour Mill.

The Island Road had only been recently built. Previous to that, where the road runs now was part of green pasture and woodland "let as town parks on long leases, and inaccessible to the public". Originally it was called Island Strand, and extended, a long level stretch, from Irish Street corner to the Bridge; but the railway engineers had to raise the level considerably to make the present Railway Hill. In 1846 there were only a few houses on the river side of the road, while almost from the River Lane to the Old Barracks, marked the boundary of a fine green space along the other side of which was the Irish Street. Here in Irish Street the Corn Market was located; there were 80 houses altogether, most of them small thatched dwellings to left and right.

Another road built shortly before 1846 was the present Wexford road. The "Bear Meadows" are mentioned later as one of the Urban boundaries; they belonged to the "Bear Inn", a celebrated local hostelry, frequently mentioned in our records. In 1798 Snowe tells us that he had the cavalry drawn up at the "Bear Inn" before the attack of the Insurgents.

A hundred years ago the Shannon was much more thickly populated than in our time. On Shannon Hill alone there were no fewer that 240 rated premises, mostly small thatched houses. In addition there were 30 houses in Drumgoold, 12 on Craheen road and 32 at Killagoley Lane (Springvalley); and also on Wood Lane, leading from Shannon Hill across towards Hurstbourne Road, were 15 small dwellings, all trace of which has long since been obliterated. The present St Senan's Road had not been built; and in Templeshannon and Old Church — one continuous thoroughfare — there were 58 buildings, mostly dwellings-houses, but including many stores, and a large malting concern (Thompson's). On Templeshannon Quay were numerous stores, a large Steam Mill (Cullen's) and a Store and Kiln (Robert Sparrow). On Shannon Hill, we find mention of two large stores and kilns

(Ryan's and Stackhouse's), and a malt-house, kiln and yard (P. J. Roche).

The street then called Duffry Street ran from Duffry Gate to the corner of Irish Street — thus including the Cathedral Street and Main Street of our day. The thoroughfare from the top of Irish Street across Market Square to the top of Castle Hill was then known as Market Street.

Enniscorthy of a century ago could not be described as an industrial town; in fact, it contained nothing in the way of factories or large-scale manufacturing industries. Its great source of wealth consisted in those numerous smaller concerns that were scattered all over the town — small mills, malt-houses, tanneries, workshops, house-crafts, kilns and so on — each contributing its own share to the people's prosperity. We have already mentioned Freeman's Mill, and Pounder's Brewery and Mill, on Mill Park Road, and the numerous larger premises on the Shannon side of the river. In Maguire's Lane there were two Tanneries (Thomas Sinnott) and a Foundry (the proprietor was Arthur Kavanagh; the name survives on the present iron gate of the Vinegar Hill tower). There were several woolstores, brick yards, and small bacon curing premises. Lewis mentions that the town had a rope factory.

In Barrack Street was a store, malt-house and kiln (William Moran) with a high valuation, and another kiln (R. Joyce); while other small malting concerns were to be found at Friary Hill (James Moran), on the Duffry Gate, in Maudlins Folly and two on the Shannon side; Edward Askins was the proprietor of a tannery in Wafer Street and a workshop in Rafter Street. In Mary Street there were two kilns and several stores; lime was burned extensively in the proximity of the quays, while a score of places could be named as the site of forges since fallen into disuse.

Freeman's Flour and Corn Mill was also a flannel mill. "The weaving of flannel is carried on here," we learn in 1843, "and the flannel is sold on the streets of the town." Pounder's was a brewery, as well as a corn and flour mill; the mill wheel was 34 feet in diameter. Nicholas Sinnot had a new corn store and timber yard quite close to the river; at Salthouse Lane, John Hinton had yet a bigger store, and here "a few yards of canal from the stone wall to the river is made for boats". The new Market Shambles were in Friary Lane; there were 31 stalls, but only a third of these were occupied.

Then there were the small housecrafts and trades. The textiles trades alone must have given employment to a considerable numbers of works — weavers, dressers and spinners, bonnet makers, milliners, seamstresses, and so on. A good deal could be written about the extensive flax-growing and linen industry that existed here, until its decline in the late nineteenth century. There were a number of woollen and cotton mills in the neighbourhood. In the town over a dozen nailers hammered their busy trade; numerous chandlers (principally around Castle Street) plied their craft, and the coopers, coachmakers, shoemakers, broguemakers, cabinetmakers, and such skilled craftsmen. In addition, large numbers earned their livelihood at the building crafts — even as late as 1881 the town had 39 carpenters, 26 masons, 6 slaters and 10 plasters. In the same year we find that there were 16 painters, 41 tailors and 50 bakers here.

A study of any street throws an interesting light on the trades and occupations of the people. The houses in Slaney Street in 1843 included the following: Three grocers, six shoemakers, a baker, a seedsman, a victualler, two apothecaries, a cabinet-maker, a school-master (John Kenny), a printer and bookbinder (John Pilkington), a woollen draper, two confectioners, a leather seller, a saddler, three provision stores and a straw milliner. Joseph Carroll had a hotel at Slaney Place. At Main Street, John Ward was the proprietor of another hotel; he had also a holding at Convent Road which included a "coach house and a winnowing house". There was a carver and gilder (James White) in Church Street; in Court Street lived William Mooney, whose trade was that of gunsmith, and whose name is prominent in the Young Ireland movement; Alexander Murphy was a brickmaker in Weafer Street; straw bonnet-makers were numerous; the names of some of the chandlers were: Thomas

Moran, Catherine Jordan, Nicholas Holinsworth, John Robinson, John Nolan (opposite the Cathedral), and James Farrell, at Duffry Gate.

Many of these house-crafts have faded completely from the life of the district, all of them have suffered seriously as the century passed. The advent of the factory era, and their inability to survive against the highly-organised competition of foreign mass-production, led to their decline.

Here brief mention may be made of the numerous mills that flourished in the neighbourhood of Enniscorthy a century ago. Besides the larger flour-mills, owned by the Davis family at St John's, Kilcarbery and Fairfield, there were no less than forty small mills within a radius of a dozen miles. Ballinaslaney, Edermine, Ballymotey, Cooladine, Garrybrit, Boolabawn, Monart, Tomgarrow, Ballinglae — to mention only a few — were the centres of small corn-mills, while corn and carding mills were going full blast at Blackwater and Mohurry. There were woollen mills at Monart and Inch (Blackwater). Clohamon had a small flax and corn mill, together with Lewis' large cotton factory, when the village comprised of 49 houses. Some of these mills still survive but most of them, like the vanished villages of Wexford, are no more.

During the 1840s, Enniscorthy was in the anomalous position that it was without any form of local government. The townspeople had little cause to lament the passing in 1840 of the old system of rule by Portreeve and Burgesses, who had continued in office even after the disfranchisement of the borough by the Act of Union. It was not till February, 1851, that Town Commissioners were established, their duties limited to "the lighting, cleansing and watching of the town". In November the first Town Rate was struck, providing for a total annual outlay of £94 7s. I0d., of which £55 was for gas lighting. Premises of less than £5 valuation were exempt, and the rate for valuation over £5, £10, and £20 was 4d., 6d. and 8d. respectively. In June, 1855 the Commissioners gave place to a new body, with the same title, but with much wider functions. The salary of the Clerk was £15 and that of the Streets Inspector £10. Looking over the century, and the changes that occurred in local administration, there was only one civic office that continued in unbroken succession throughout, that of Bellman, those quaint figures, of whom it might be truly said that they held their unofficial appointment by popular acclamation. They played an important part in the life of the town, performing manifold services, traversing the streets with bell in hand for the auction and the fair, for the pageant and the play, for property lost and found and a thousand other things. From beginning to end of the century we meet them — in the pages of Kennedy they're mentioned, down to one of the last and best-loved of them all, of whom it is recorded that he announced with thunderous voice from Enniscorthy Bridge the sinking fortunes of France in the Franco-Prussian War. Nothing, perhaps, is so frequently remembered in the conversation of old people as the exploits and eccentricities of these many-sided personages.

In April, 1851, the Commissioners defined the Town Boundary. It went on a line from St John's Bridge around to Bellefield Gate to Moyne turn (to Greenville) — to Weir Style Stream on the Dublin Road — crossing the River to Rectory Gate on the Solsboro Road — to Drumgoold Cross Roads — to "Bear Meadows Gate". At a subsequent meeting in the same month, these limits were considered to extend too far and were altered to radiate in each direction to a limit of 80 perches from the Market Square, thus coming into close accord with the present boundary. The principle points mentioned are: (1) The south end of the store lately used as a Workhouse on the Wexford Road; (2) The Angle at John Doyle's Forge in Templeshannon Street; (3) North corner of Templeshannon graveyard; (4) The north boundary wall of Murphy's Livery Stables yard on Island Road and Irish Street; (5) Back Yard Gate of Rose Hill House on Nunnery Road; (6) Gate of Richard Sparrow's concern at Duffry Gate; (7) Gateway to Edward Askin's land on Ross Road; (8) South end wall of Peter Rowe's House in Guttle Street; (9) South Wall Salt House Lane on Mill Park Road.

Street lighting was first introduced in January, 1852, when twenty public lamps were erected by the gas company, in accordance with their contract with the Town Commissioners. Portion of the advertisement inviting tenders read as follows:

> "To light the Town of Enniscorthy with Coal Gas, the lighting of the lamps to commence at dusk, and all to be put out by daybreak — From 1 May to 15 August each year, and the five bright nights of each moon, to be excepted."

In October of that year, the Commissioners decided to reconsider the location of the lamps and to increase their number. A special meeting for that purpose was held on October 4, and the new sites were selected, but apparently the Commissioners considered it prudent to wait till darkness, for the contemporary record says: "Resolved — That the selection of sites for the nine lamps be deferred to this night at the News-Room ... At half-past seven o'clock the Commissioners again assembled, and having carefully examined the town in darkness, agreed that the lights to be added to those already in the town be placed as follows:

> 1 In Irish Street at Cornmarket.
> 1 On Templeshannon Quay.
> 1 In Black Street (on Joe Weatherell's house).
> 1 At Duffry Gate between the Chapel and William Lee's corner.
> 1 Between Peter Dixon's and James Malone's house in Market Square."

What a strange sight it must have been as the Commissioners — eighteen in number — went in a body through narrow lanes and alleys, picking their steps in the darkness of an October night, discharging their public duties. Names long and honourably linked with Enniscorthy's life — names of families still happily with us — are in this list — Bernard O'Flaherty (chairman), William Moran, Edward

Askins, Matthew Furlong, Myles Doran. Many of the names, too, are no longer familiar in our midst — Keohler and Bobiar, Hinton and Nelson, Nuzum and Cranfield — our ruler in a past generation.

It may be added that one of the first public lamps erected was opposite the Cathedral gate. Each light cost £2 15s. per annum. Gas lighting continued in the town till the Urban Council, in 1924, introduced its own Electricity Scheme, which later became incorporated in the National Electricity undertaking.

During the greater part of the nineteenth century the townspeople relied for their water supply on spring wells, a goodly number of which were situated in the town and its environs. This source was supplemented in the 1830s, when pipes were laid down bringing water from Sheill's Well in Templeshannon to the west side. At this time the bridge was widened and lowered. Three fountains were supplied from these pipes. Later, two pumps and three fountains, supplied from other sources, were added. In 1867 mention is made of a plan to build a reservoir at the Bishop's Well Field to supply the western side with soft water, but apparently it came to nothing. Following the construction of the railway tunnel, some of the spring wells were closed, the replaced by new fountains. In 1891 the Town Commissioners erected the new Reservoir at Drumgoold, costing £2,800.

We have already referred to the flourishing business carried on by the merchants engaged in the corn and butter trade, in provisions and general merchandise, as well as milliners and drapers — hardworking, enterprising traders, who contributed in such large measure to the town's development and growth. There had been excellent crops in 1843 and 1844, and we are told that in spite of the bad land system, agricultural methods were improving, a fact which was attributed by a local landholder to "better manuring, deeper ploughing, earlier cropping and greater attention to renewing seed". All this reflected itself in the commercial prosperity which undoubtedly existed here in the years before the Great Famine. Yet, at the same period, we find ample evidence to show that there existed lamentable conditions of poverty amongst large sections of the people. That is the paradox with which the student of social conditions is confronted.

The housing position of the poor people was appalling. A great part of the population lived in small sooty thatched cabins, with mud floors. There were almost 400 dwellings in the town, built of mud walls and containing only one room; 108 of these were on the Shannon side. A large number of the other houses were little better, though they contained more than one room. There were 1,052 houses in the town in 1841 for a population of 7,016, a figure which was being yearly augmented by the influx of families in distress, driven from their small holdings as a result of the land clearances, which were such a common feature of life here in the 1840s. Their arrival served only to add to the volume of poverty already existing. The evidence given by the local witnesses before the Devon Commission in 1844 gives us valuable information on the condition that prevailed here at that time. The clearing of the estates by rack-renting landlords, the drift into the town, the poverty of the cottiers and labourers, the reluctance of even the most distressed to enter the Union Workhouse, which had been built in 1842, the simple unvaried diet of the people — all these facts are brought out clearly, together with those fundamental faults of the system of land tenure, which were the ruin of Irish prosperity. One is struck by the absence of decent hospital services. "How children are provided for on the death of their parents it is most difficult to say," said an Enniscorthy witness, "they are very badly off, and are often scattered about the world as best they can find shelter or employment".

The rate of agricultural wages in the district at that time was 10d. per day without diet; 5d. with diet. In the town, wages rates were only slightly higher; and one is astonished at the low rates paid to tradesmen, nine and ten shillings weekly being frequently mentioned. The level of urban wages can be judged from the interesting item of news that in 1845 a tender was accepted to draw stones from St John's to the Union grounds at the rate of 8d. per ton! It must be remembered, of course, that commodity prices were also very low. Coal could then be landed on the Quay at less than £1 per ton; in 1844 it was 15s. 6d. The local tanners could supply best heavy butt leather at 10d. per lb., light at 8d; and best brogue slitter at 11d. Glass could be bought at 2d. per full diamond square; salt was 1s. 6d. per cwt. Dressed flax was 8½d. per lb., while Coolamain bleaching green could bleach linen at a penny per yard.

Food prices were equally low; milk was a penny a pint and potatoes could generally be bought on the market at less than 3d. a stone, at a time when the potato constituted an essential element in the food of the people. Meat then was an infrequent luxury. Earlier in the century, Fraser mentions that in North Wexford "they generally have potatoes three times a day as long as they last, which in good years is generally until the new potatoes come in". Hickey says that meat was a luxury which seldom falls to the people's share, except at Christmas and Easter. Another writer supports this, saying that the food "is generally potatoes and milk, with some changes on festival days," a fact which is clearly brought out by the Devon Commission witnesses.

In 1836, Rev. James Roche, Adm., supplied to the Commission of Enquiry on the Relief of the Poor certain information on conditions in Enniscorthy. Of the houses in the town, only 300 could be described as good. About 120 new houses had been built during the past three years, he said, the average annual rent being £2 10s. to £3. The tenants of these new houses were for the most part "broken farmers and beggars". The population of the town had been increasing since 1832; there were no manufactures; the labourers were employed on the land, on road-building, and some at a distillery. He referred to the fact that children were sent to do casual or light work about the age of twelve. The food of labourers and working tradesmen was potatoes, milk, herrings principally; some tradesmen had meat occasionally. The Distillery mentioned by Fr Roche was at Island Strand, on the site of the present Maltings.

To the student of local history, the old account books of local merchants can be a valuable source of information. They give a very intimate picture of social conditions, detailing commodity prices, showing changing food habits and standards of living and reflecting the gradual introduction of imported luxury goods. Mr Michael J. Jordan, Market Square, was kind enough to place at my disposal a large day-book for 1863-5 for the extensive business carried on by his family, established over a century ago. Prices generally are very much lower than those of the present day. Notable exception is tea, then 3s. 4d. per lb., which by then had begun to establish itself as the most popular of household beverages; sugar, too, was very dear at 5s. l0d. a stone. Drinks were cheap — whiskey, 4s. 4d. a quart; stout and ale, 2d. a bottle. Tobacco was 4s. a lb., and pipes 2d. a dozen! Three dozen pipes and one dozen covers could be retailed at 7½d.! Candle sales are set down as follow: 1lb. wax candles, 2s.; 1lb composite candles, 1s.; 1 lb. mound candles, 7d.; 1 lb. dipt candles, 6d., the latter types being supplied by the local chandlers at a time when the rushlight holder and resin snab were still familiar objects in Wexford households.

Mr Patrick Clifford was kind enough to give me valuable information, taken from old notebooks in his possession, on prices and wages in the building trade. In 1856 the wages of labourers did not exceed 1s. 6d. a day, while tradesmen received 3s. per day. Lime was 2s.2d. per barrel, sand 1s. a load; eight-penny nails were 4d. per hundred. Of course, working hours in those days were very long — 12 and 13 hours a day were the normal order. The workers in Freeman's and Pounder's Mills in 1843 worked 13 hours a day throughout the year.

As the century progressed we take note of the gradual rise in wages, and shortening of working hours, accompanied by a fall in the purchasing power of money. The town's prosperity, shattered by the Great Famine, recovered partially in the 1850s, and for the remainder of the century ebbed and flowed with the varying fortunes of the agricultural industry. The population declined steadily, for the flood of emigration continued in full surge. Housing conditions improved gradually; most of the old unhealthy dwellings were replaced by better-class houses; and in this connection it may be mentioned that not least of the many splendid services rendered to Enniscorthy by Fr James A. Cullen, during his period in the House of Missions, was his work towards the betterment of housing in the Shannon. Looking back over the century, there is undoubtedly a very marked improvement in the standard of living of the people, especially of the poor. In our own day a native Irish Parliament has made the provision of excellent cheap dwellings for the people, the building of a modern hospital system, and the development of social services to aid the poor and needy, a first charge upon the nation's purse. The work done by the County Wexford Board of Health between 1922-42 deserves special mention for its splendid contribution to social improvement, the results of which are everywhere evident.

∛

"Seldom has a nation experienced so definite an ending-point and a starting-point in its history as Ireland had in the Great Famine," says a modern historian. In towns like ours, the memory of that tragic landmark — "Black 1847" — has lived in tradition, and even if it had never been mentioned in written records or taught in school-rooms, it could never be forgotten. It is only when we view the building of the Cathedral against the stark background of the Famine years, that we can properly appreciate the spirit of enduring faith and generous sacrifice, of the men and women who walked these streets a century ago. In 1843, when the foundation stone was laid, here was a town enjoying a fair prosperity; by June, 1846, when Mass was first celebrated in the partly-finished structure, the town was already on the threshold of the great catastrophe.

The first news of its coming to Enniscorthy is met with in the late summer of 1845, when the Guardians of Enniscorthy Union found it difficult to obtain supplies of potatoes. The supply position improved in the Autumn, but it was then found that the potatoes were tainted and big quantities had to be destroyed. As the winter approached, it became extremely difficult to obtain adequate supplies, and on several occasions the Union dietary had to be altered to substitute other foods for potatoes. On November 7 the Guardians called the attention of the Government to "the lamentable increase in distress consequent upon the disease of the potato crop". In the beginning of December detailed reports were submitted from all over the district from clergymen and public representatives describing the serious failure of the crop in each parish. On December 5, 1845, a full meeting of the Guardians was held to consider the position. At this meeting a comprehensive set of proposals was put before the British Government on the suggestion of Mr John Maher, Ballinkeele, a series of proposals which, if adopted, would have entirely prevented the great calamities that befell the country in the following year. These proposals, circulated to every public body in Ireland, advocated "the establishment of a Board of Public Safety, out of the machinery of the Poor Law Act, and the advancement on the security of a rate (to be raised by each Board) of a sum adequate to meet necessity of the case". Printed by Page, the local printer, these proposals show with great clarity the position in Enniscorthy on the threshold of the great Famine. It mentions the abundance of the corn crops, and the high price of market produce, and laments that "the labourers and cottier farmers are likely to be subjected to great privation and misery in being obliged to purchase food in the markets during Spring". Incidentally, the document mentions that "the calamity has been less in this Union than in the other parts of Ireland".

The winter of 1845 passed with some distress, but no widespread destitution. It was only in the early Autumn of 1846 that the real tragedy commenced, for the blight had appeared again, and the entire potato crop was a failure.

From this date, the chronicle of the months becomes a diary of distress. Gradually rice, Indian meal and oatmeal were introduced into the dietary in place of potatoes.

It is not often that the replies to an official query mean so much in human suffering as the following from the Clerk of Enniscorthy Union to the Poor Law Commissioners:

13 AUGUST, 1846 —

(1) Has the Potato Disease
re-appeared in your Union?   (1) Yes.

(2) If yes, in how many electoral
divisions has it appeared?   (2) In all.

(3) In what electoral divisions has it
not appeared?   (3) None.

(4) What proportion of the
crop has been affected in   (4) The Whole.
your Union?

(5) For how many months
consumption would the   (5) Impossible to
healthy portion of the crop   say, as they are
supply food?   rapidly decaying.

The Board failed to obtain potato contracts, and the Union officials were ordered to obtain potatoes in the local market. Then, on 25 September, 1846, we read the ominous sentence — "On the Master's report of the total impossibility of procuring potatoes in the market of Enniscorthy — it was ordered that the Rice and Indian meal dinners be extended to four days per week in future" — a piece of information that reflects the distress that must have existed in the town at this date. In October the Board urges the necessity of starting a sewerage scheme "with a view to having it instantly commenced during this period of distress and want of employment of the labouring classes". In the last week of Autumn 1846, the Public Works commenced in Enniscorthy.

Meanwhile winter was approaching, a Relief Committee of public-spirited citizens was set up in the town to alleviate distress. Food prices rose rapidly. In October, 1845, oatmeal was supplied to the Guardians at £12 10s. per ton. In January, 1846, the price was £15 10s. while in November, 1846, it was £20 5s., and in 1847 still higher. Similarly, a 4lb. loaf supplied in the beginning of 1845 for 5½d. cost 8½d. by Christmas, 1846. Wages were low, food dear and scarce — hunger began to tell its tale, the Famine Fever was raging. On November 6 it is reported that there were 606 people in the Union Workhouse where in September, 1845, there were only 271. Within ten days the number was over 700, rising to 758 on December 5. The situation was becoming desperate. Schoolrooms were converted into wards and yet with the increased accommodation, the Guardians found it impossible to meet the needs of the unfortunate poor. Just a fortnight before Christmas 1846, the Board had to inform the large number of applicants for admission "that, in consequence of the present numbers in the House, we are under the very painful necessity of totally refusing all applications for admission about to come before us this day". The Board went on to consider the possibility of building sheds or taking houses "for the admission of the great numbers of destitute poor applying weekly". Meanwhile, we read "of the great pressure at Mr Davis's mill for Indian meal".

The *Nation* newspaper, in its issue of Christmas week, 1846, quoted from the *Wexford Independent* the following description of conditions in North Wexford:

"Our accounts from the northern parts of the county are most deplorable. What the poor people earn on the Public Works is barely sufficient to supply them. All their earnings go for food, and the consequence is that they have nothing left to procure clothing. Since the extreme cold set in, sickness and death have accordingly followed in its train. Inflammation of the lungs, fevers and other maladies resulting from excessive privation, have been bearing away their victims. Many died in the course of last week, and the illness in every case was traceable to the want of clothing, if not of sufficient food."

Again, in January, 1847, the Guardians were forced to reject all applications for admission. The Fever Hospital was also overcrowded and fever patients were being admitted to the Workhouse in large numbers, while the local Relief Committee was doing its utmost to provide extra accommodation for these victims of the fever, and cooked meals for the destitute poor.

In February, 1847 the Famine distress reached such a pitch that the Guardians found the Workhouse entirely inadequate and commenced to take over Auxiliary Workhouses in various parts of the town to accommodate the large number of applicants; some cottages were also taken over and permanent additions made to the old building. On February 12 the first Auxiliary Workhouse was occupied; it was store-house in Irish Street; the second was rented at the Duffry Gate in March, capable of accommodating 200 between them. In November a third was opened at Templeshannon, intended to house 200 children, while altogether eight such Auxiliaries were occupied, the others being at Friary Lane, Guttle Street, The Quay, Templeshannon No. 2 and Duffry Gate No. 2.

It was only in the spring of 1847 that the Famine was entering its period of climax. Early in March the Poor Law Commissioners report that "the Workhouse now presents a scene of confusion, which could only be aggravated by the presence of contagious disease, by which the establishment is hourly threatened". Each week brought fresh news of distress; people crowded into the new Auxiliaries; the Fever Hospital became overcrowded, and the Authorities had to make hurried arrangements for the provision of additional hospital accommodation. Even then, in June, 1847, the

Guardians were forced to discharge from the Workhouse large numbers of inmates in order "to provide accommodation for poor persons labouring under fever". They, at the same time, gave bedding and furniture to the Enniscorthy Relief Committee, who had hired a new building for the fever patients then unprovided for. Meanwhile, expenditure mounted, and the Union was called upon to provide from the rates a sum of over £15,000 (including expenses under the Temporary Relief Act) where £2,750 was adequate in 1845.

This terrible tragedy continued right on to the end of 1847, and although the climax had by then been reached, the distressful consequences are evident for several years afterwards. As late as 1851 there were still 1,640 people in the Workhouse, and three of the Auxiliaries still open. There was little sign of a return to normal prosperity. When steps were taken in that year to establish Town Commissioners there was strong support for the viewpoint expressed in the following resolution:

> "That in consequence of the depression in every branch of trade and business in this town, and no appearance of any return to our former state of prosperity, we deem it highly imprudent to agree to any amount of taxation whatever."

We see evidence of decay also in the large amount struck off for irrecoverable rates for small houses down or untenanted, or "where no effects are to be had". Towards the end of 1852 the remaining Auxiliaries — those at Templeshannon and Guttle Street — were closed; and we find many workers still employed at road-building. At Christmas, 1851, work was in progress on the new Kiltealy-Ballycarney line.

And so the country lay prostrate after the Famine. Nothing in our history, perhaps, fills us with so much pity and sorrow; pity for the poor of our country, for it was they who suffered most; no other event leaves us with so much to reflect on and wonder at — how, for instance, an ignoble ascendancy stood idly by and watched the export of great quantities of corn, exported to pay rents to absentee landlords, corn which might have saved a million lives. Tradition points to the spots where the Famine victims were laid to rest; and one shudders to imagine in grim realism all the sad scenes that became so familiar during those months — the hunger and distress, the ravages of the fever, the break-up of happy homesteads, the mass burials — all the heart-rending incidents that few writers have found heart to fully describe. It is indeed little wonder that the word "Famine" has lingered on in our tradition like the memory of an earthly hell.

଼

July, 1848! Only a few weeks ago John Mitchel was transported. It is a few minutes past five on a Saturday evening. Here comes the Dublin Mail Coach, jaunting noisily over the roughly-paved surface of the bridge. At Rudd's Hotel it stops, and out steps a passenger who, all the long journey down from Dublin, had been turning in his mind a thought which had occurred to many Irishmen, the thought of armed revolt. It is the magnificent and gallant figure of Smith O'Brien. The word goes round that it is he. A small crowd gathers. The peelers watch him closely. But he does not linger long in the streets — it is a town torn by the tragedy of Famine — he leaves to spend the night with his friend, John Maher, at Ballinkeele.

Meanwhile, things happen rapidly in Dublin. The Habeas Corpus Act is suspended. A warrant is issued for O'Brien's arrest. John Blake Dillon and Thomas Francis Meagher join the Wexford night coach a few miles outside the city, and follow O'Brien to Enniscorthy. They arrive at five in the morning. Meagher tells the story in his Recollections:

> "At Rudd's Hotel we dismounted and ordered a car for Ballinkeele. It was little more than five o'clock and the morning was bitterly cold. A clear bright sun, however, was changing into golden vapour the grey

mist, which arched the gentle current of the Slaney.
Not a soul was stirring in the streets; the hotel itself
was dismally quiet; the fowls in the stable yard, and
the gruff old dog, beside the warm ashes of the
kitchen fire, were all at rest."

They travelled to Ballinkeele and conferred with Smith
O'Brien. He agreed with them that armed revolt was now the
only honourable course.

Having breakfasted, the three Confederate leaders
returned to Enniscorthy. Dillon and Meagher attended Mass
in the Cathedral. Before their departure for Kilkenny they
held a conference in the house of a leading Confederate, and
addressed a big crowd that had gathered in the Main Street.
We can easily picture the eagerness of that crowd and guess
where their sympathies lay. Meagher tells us that the people
pledged themselves to join in the Rising when they heard of
fighting going on in Kilkenny and Tipperary. But 1848
passed without any Rising in Wexford, for the great Famine
had at once demonstrated the need for active resistance, and
destroyed the strength necessary to sustain it.

When Smith O'Brien was put on trial at the Clonmel
Assizes, one of the principal documents relied on by the
Crown against him was the address of welcome presented to
him by the Enniscorthy men. In this very interesting address,
they said "That they had seen with lively indignation the
atrocious tyranny exercised by the Government in the
transportation of John Mitchel, the bravest of the brave," and
concluded with this rather seditious sentence: "They have
long felt the oppression and insolence of the Government to
be well-nigh intolerable, and they would, for their own part,
be well-content to put a speedy end to this tyranny for ever
at the cost of their lives."

The 1848 Rising ended in failure. To an Enniscorthy
person it is a source of pride that by the brief visit of the
leaders here, the town is associated with yet another national
uprising.

If we could walk in the midst of those patriotic kinsmen of ours, who welcomed Smith O'Brien to Enniscorthy in 1848 we would see old men, with vivid recollection of 1798, standing side by side with younger men, who lived on to the days of Rossa and the Fenians, and saw the failure of another Rising. These younger men handed on the tradition; they joined with the men of a new generation in keeping the spirit of nationality alive in defiance of an unrelenting tyranny.

അ

Brief account must be given of Catholic education here before the coming of the great Teaching Orders. A traveller through County Wexford in 1812 describes for us a journey on foot from Bunclody to New Ross. "We found many weavers spread through the cottages," he says, "and the ever-cheerful sound of the shuttle often enlivened the way." He speaks of the education and schools he finds on his journey. He laments the scarcity of suitable text-books in the Irish and English languages for these schools "which we observed at all the chapels as we walked along and education attended to very generally".

All over the county "the school beside the chapel" was to be found. Side by side with these were the hedge-schoolmasters and poor scholars, some of whose names survive in tradition. There is nothing more inspiring in our local history than the story of these schools and schoolmasters, who, with the aid of a faithful Catholic people, kept the traditional Irish learning alive, in the teeth of a bitter and bigoted opposition. It is one aspect of our past that deserves closer study.

In 1835 Denis Noolan kept a Hedge School at Monart, and Moses Doyle at Scoby. Another of these schools was established in Templeshanbo Parish by Patrick Keating in the previous year; his programme was "Spelling, Reading, Writing, Arithmetic, Grammar, Book-keeping, Geometry and Latin". At Monart Mill, in 1826, Martin Breen taught a school "in a house of stone and mud".

In the town, in 1826 — the year the first of the Teaching Orders, the Presentation Order, came — there were 156 boys attending the school in the Cathedral Yard in a "Schoolhouse in an unfinished state," supported by the subscriptions of the people, with Dr Keating as patron. The teacher was Owen Nolan, whose salary was £24 a year. In another room in the same building, 152 girls were educated by Bridget McDonnell, who received £18 per annum. The Presentation Nuns then undertook the task of teaching the girls in their new school. By 1843 the Nuns had transferred from Weafer Street to the present Convent Road site; in that year the schoolroom and chapel were one house, the upper storey used as a chapel, and the lower as a schoolroom. In 1835 the Convent had 230 pupils. In the same year, 196 boys were attending the "Chapel School", the teacher then being Martin Dwyer. This school building in the Cathedral Grounds (where the Christian Brothers taught for a brief period in later years) was an important centre for Catholic gatherings. Meetings of the Repeal Association were held there; the members of the local Workers' Savings Bank, or Friendly Society (St Patrick's Society) met there; it was used later as a Reading Room and Band Room; old survivors recall taking part in plays there.

Together with the schools already mentioned, there were many other Catholic Schoolmasters, each with his own curriculum, throughout the town. Thomas Kennedy, at Irish Street, taught 60 pupils in a house of stone, clay and mortar; in Back Street, a teacher called McCurtin taught almost 80 children "Reading, Writing, Arithmetic, Grammar, Book-keeping and Catholic Catechism" for 6s. 6d. to 10s. 6d. a quarter; while Anthony O'Hara had his Classical and Commercial School in Guttle Street in a slated house built of bricks. There were three small schools for Catholic girls in Weafer Street; the teachers were Mrs Clifford, Elizabeth Walsh and Catherine Redmond; of two of these schools it is recorded that they were conducted "in a small room in a cabin". Elizabeth Doyle in Guttle Street and Mrs Cook in Devereaux Lane had large classes in small houses — again described as "a small room in a cabin".

In The Shannon, James Roche taught 40 pupils in a mud-walled thatched house, and in Drumgoold, Thomas Bryan had his school in a building of similar type. The yearly earnings of Thomas Bryan are given as £10. In 1835 two Catholic Schoolmasters at The Shannon were John Mallet and Thomas Connor, the latter receiving 2d. to 4d. a week from each pupil. We have the names of other Catholic Schoolteachers in the town in the same year — Michael Nolan, who, for 2d. and 3d. a week from each pupil, taught Grammar, Geography and Book-keeping, in addition to the Three R's, Mensuration and Catechism; while Martin Hughes and Miss Tobin are also mentioned. In 1826 the parish school for the Protestant population was conducted in the Market House, and supported by an annual contribution of £20 from the Earl of Portsmouth; and in 1835 the Market House was used for Presbyterian Services.

Edward Gannon taught school in an extensive house in Main Street (opposite the Cathedral Gate) in the 1840s. John Kenny, in Slaney Street, and Thomas Masterson, in Court Street, were other schoolmasters of that period. In Weafer Street, John O'Meagher conducted a Boarding and Day School, in the house owned by Dr Keating at Weafer Street, where the Presentation Nuns first lived.

og

Thursday was market day in Enniscorthy, but corn and butter were brought to the market daily. A particular street was allocated by traditional usage to each type of produce on the market, and while the local authorities tried at various times to alter these, their orders were frequently disregarded. The corn market, for instance, was at Irish Street, the fowl market at Abbey Square, and the egg and butter market at Castle Street corner.

If you talk to the older generation, they'll tell you the dates of the old monthly fairs of Enniscorthy — January 20, February 21, and right through the months to the Christmas Fair on St Thomas's Day (December 21). Two factors helped to increase the importance of these fairs from the 1860s onwards — the transition from tillage to pasture and the building of the railway. From this time the cattle and horse fairs grew in size. The fairs of those days, besides being great centres for buying and selling, were also established social institutions. The Market Square was the liveliest centre in a busy town. On the centre of the rough, sloping street, were piled ladders, gates and troughs; the dealing men, in their booths and stands, were loudly advertising their wares, while round the flagged footpaths the town merchants displayed their goods. Scattered round the Square in the places allotted to them by custom were the seasonable products — firkins of butter, baskets of eggs, loads of potatoes and cabbage plants, boxes of herrings, cart-loads of lime, packs of wool — and at the foot of Wafer Street were gathered the brogue-makers, with their kishes of brogues. October brought the Onion Fair and November the Apple Fair. Through the thronged streets on these Fair Days roved the pedlar, the juggler and the quack. Here, too, gathered the ballad-singers, singing the popular "Come-all-Yes" and street ballads that told of joys and sorrows, of love and liberty, eviction and exile, Redcoats and Rapparees.

That fine ballad, "The Bantry Girl's Lament", calls to mind the celebrated Fair of Moneyhore:

> *"The boys will miss you sorely when*
> *Moneyhore comes round,*
> *And grieve that their bould captain is*
> *nowhere to be found."*

Moneyhore, Mohurry, Clohamon, Scarawalsh — the passing of a century has brought an end to these old village fairs and has lent to them a romantic glow which will linger on in popular memory long after the dates of the gatherings and the locations of the greens are forgotten.

Space permits mention of only a few of the great social gatherings and sports of past generations — the Regattas and

Athletic meetings, Agricultural Shows and early coursing fixtures, the Races of Drumgoold; and, belonging to a much earlier period, the Races of Ballyhogue, still remembered in tradition and recorded in the pages of Kennedy and Ogle. The Circus, too, was a memorable event — the shouts of the children brought out the older people to see the Circus Procession pass, with colour and clamour, full retinue of wagons, ponies and horses, clowns and acrobats, dwarfs and giants, moving in state to the blare of the bandsmen. Highlight of the display, says an Island Road veteran, was the Tall Man, in motley garb, striding triumphantly on stilts from street to street, towering over the low eaves of the thatched houses and tapping playfully the upper windows of the new two-storied slated dwellings. In the late nineteenth century the Circus ground was at Mill Park Road, in a field beside the river, before the present houses were built. It was also held at "Hayes' Field," since taken over as a housing site, on the town side of Bellefield Gaelic Grounds. This field, which was once specially prepared for use as a Fair Green but never used for that purpose, was the scene of many fine athletic encounters, including a thrilling bicycle race when the Penny-farthing design was first introduced. It was in the present Bellefield Grounds that the famous John Mangan, of Kilmuckridge, on a July evening in 1900, set up a world's record by throwing the 56lbs. weight a distance of 15 feet, ¾ inches over the bar.

Throughout the century there was a continual inflow of people to the town from the surrounding rural district. This was more than offset by the steady drain of emigration which had its origin in the Famine distress and which has not ceased even in our own day. Dublin, and the great industrial cities of Great Britain, were the destination of many, while the majority went to the United States and Canada. Australia and the Argentine attracted a lesser number. An advertisement published by a local shipping agent in 1872 gives the passage to New York and Quebec as six guineas. Other ports mentioned include St John's, Buenos Aires, Baltimore, Boston, Melbourne, Sydney; he concludes in bold type:

"Thousands of emigrants have been forwarded
through the Agency of the undersigned, without any
accident, to every part of the world."

Earlier in the century, Wexford emigrants went in large
numbers to Quebec. Some years before the Famine the fare
for steerage passengers from New Ross to Quebec was £2, in
addition to which the emigrant had to bring with him
equipment and provisions for the voyage, the average length
of which was five weeks. The sea-journey was generally one
of great hardship for the emigrants for often times the ships
on which they travelled were the rough vessels employed on
the timber trade to Upper Canada. In 1852, when a party of
three adults and three children were arranging to travel from
Enniscorthy to Toronto, a sum of £17 was "deemed sufficient
to locate them in Toronto". A scheme of assisted emigration
of destitute people to British America was to a limited extent.
The expenses of one emigrant from here to Quebec in March,
1846, are given as follows: Total, £7 5s.; made up of passage,
£2 5s., provisions, £1 15s.; clothes and bedding, £2 5s.; for
contingencies on landing, £1. Emigration did not take place
between September and March, as ships were not considered
safe within that period.

Over the years then, there have been many changes. It
has, taken generally, been a period of growth and
development; we have seen, especially in our own time, a
notable advance in social well-being. Much has undoubtedly
been achieved; but a great deal more remains to be done. We
will be pardoned for expressing the hope that if the town is
in future years subjected to that modern process called
Planning, that those who are sent here to undertake the task
will respect tradition, will do nothing to destroy the town's
native dignity and simple graciousness, remembering that it
is a place full of history, of romance and teeming inspiration.

In the town of our day, too, there is much that is
picturesque and lovable. Looking down over it through the
evening mists, it takes on a medieval character, grey, placid,
restful; it seems like something that has wandered out of the
glamorous past, across the silent centuries, fragrant with the

memories of their passing. In how many hearts, some in far-off lands, this "kindly spot, this friendly town" means Home, with all the magic that simple word conveys! It is true that time has brought its changes, but as we look down from the hill above, we are impressed by so much that has not changed; from here all the yesterdays, to-days and to-morrows seem to merge into that timeless stream that we call Tradition. And we pray that as the "years like great black oxen tread the world", they may leave their footmark lightly here, sparing so much that is old and good and beautiful.

രു

500th ANNIVERSARY OF THE COMING OF THE FRANCISCANS TO ENNISCORTHY

The year 1960 marks the 500th anniversary of the coming of the Franciscans to Enniscorthy. In the year 1460 a monastery was established "on the edge of the river that is called Slaney" for Friars Minor of the Strict Observance. In that year the Franciscan Friary of Enniscorthy was built by Dónal Riach Kavanagh, King of Leinster, grandson of Art MacMurrough Kavanagh. An ancient Missal belonging to the monastery stated that the Friary was dedicated to the service of God on October 18, 1460. We learn from the same source that the founder of the Friary (Dónal Fuscus Lageniare, Prince of Leinster) died on April 21, 1476. The Missal was written in the monastery itself.

The Four Masters record the establishment of the Friary under the year 1460: "Mainistir Inis Corthaidh i Laighnibh in easpogoideacht Fearna ar bhru na habhann dianadh ainm Slaine do thogbhail do bhraithribh S. Froinseis." (The monastery of Enniscorthy in Leinster in the diocese of Ferns on the bank of the river that is called Slaney built for the Friars of St Francis).

More than 200 years earlier, the Norman lord, Gerald de Prendergast, had founded at St John's a Priory for Canons Regular of St Victor (Augustinians). Early in the thirteenth century the Prendergasts had established the Norman supremacy over the district and about 1230 they built Enniscorthy Castle. Both St John's Priory and the Franciscan Friary were closely associated with the castle; while St John's was a Norman foundation, the Friary established two centuries later owed its origin to the Gaelic family, the Kavanaghs. For by 1460 the Gaelic Resurgence in Leinster had reached the zenith of its triumph. The Kavanaghs had reconquered North Wexford, and Norman power was very weak outside the Pale.

The Enniscorthy Friary was one of the later houses founded by the Irish Franciscans. St Francis died in 1226, and his Order had been introduced into Ireland during the same century. The Friary in Wexford was founded about 1240, and that in New Ross before 1300.

At the time the Enniscorthy monastery extended from the site of the present Abbey Square, southwards along the river bank to include the area later covered by the premises of Enniscorthy Co-operative Agricultural Society, the Bank of Ireland, Messrs. S. and A. G. Davis and part of Lett's Brewery grounds. The church was on the site of the Bank of Ireland, and the tower further out towards the centre of Abbey Square. An Inquisition held in 1545 states that in addition to the church, "the monastery contains within its site the walls, a belfry, a Chapter house, dormitory, hall, four chambers, kitchen and other edifices two orchards and three gardens".

A sixteenth century lease speaks of "the house of Friars of Enniscorthy, with a water-mill and other appurtenances adjoining," while a rental of the same period mentions "one water-mill near the site, and one garden, together with six acres of land east of the said house". A writer describing Enniscorthy in 1537 says: "There is here a place of friars observaunts well buylded with divers old stone walls."

CB

The monastery cemetery was the burial place of the kings of Leinster, and of other noble families of the locality. The founder, Dónal Reagh, was buried there.

There is a manuscript volume preserved in the British Museum which links Enniscorthy with the tradition of Gaelic scholarship associated with the Irish Franciscans. It is a thick, small, quarto vellum manuscript, written at various periods between 1419 and 1517, containing, amongst other material, the Irish tale, the Tragic Death of Diarmaid Mac Cearbhaill. The manuscript, written in beautiful penmanship, is the work of the famous scribes, the O'Mulconrys; part of it was written in Connacht, part in Enniscorthy. The manuscript gives the date of death of the reigning King of Leinster, Art Biú Mac Dónal Riach, son of the founder of the Friary. The date of his death was St Catherine's Day, 1517.

The Friary flourished during the reign of Art Buí, and its fame is said to have overshadowed that of St John's during this period. The castle and the Friary buildings beside the river became the nucleus round which the modern town of Enniscorthy gradually grew. The Four Masters emphasise that the monastery site was beside the river — "Ar bhrú na habhann dianadh ainm Sláine."

෬

A boatman of that time travelling downstream on the Slaney from the lower tip of the Island to the Urrin mouth, would have passed in turn within easy view of the town's three most celebrated ecclesiastical foundations — Teampoll Seanáin, within a stone's throw of the river, founded by St Senan in the sixth century; the Franciscan Friary, established in the fifteenth century; and below the spot where the Urrin meets the Slaney, the Augustinian Priory of St John's between the Corrig and the riverside. Little vestige of these monastic buildings has remained to our time; little more than the place-names survive to remind us of their glorious past, symbols as they are of Enniscorthy's deep and abiding loyalty to the Faith during the Middle Ages.

The dawn of the sixteenth century saw the climax of the greatness of the Enniscorthy Friary. Before the century had gone half-way, the Enniscorthy Franciscans were to endure many sad and bitter trials and tribulations.

The Dissolution of the Monasteries by the dissolute King Henry VIII took place in 1539-40. The Friary of Enniscorthy was suppressed and in 1544 it was granted for ever to John Travers, Master of the Ordnance for "the service of a twentieth part of a knight's fee and a rent of 2s. 2d". At the same date, St John's Priory, together with the Rectory of Kilcarbery, was given to the same John Travers. An Inquisition held on August 30 of the previous year stated that "the monastery of Enniscorthy, commonly called the Friars of Enniscorthy, was founded beyond the memory of man, and was suppressed in 1539". It went on to say that "the Prior and the co-brethren have left and have relinquished claim". The jury did not know from whom the premises were held, or who the founder was. In 1552 (Feb 8) Gabriel Black was granted a lease of the site of the "late house of Friars of Enniscorthy with a watermill and other appurtenances adjoining".

Though dispossessed of their Convent, the Friars continued to live in the neighbourhood of the town for the remainder of the century. As happened in many other parts of Ireland the sons of St Francis gave invaluable assistance to the hard-pressed secular clergy during the bitter years of persecution under Queen Elizabeth I. Fr Donagh Mooney says that the Friars were scattered in the houses of their friends in the neighbourhood.

During the years 1554-58 when Mary was Queen, Catholic worship was restored in Ireland and Great Britain. The Friars re-occupied their Convent in Enniscorthy. At the time of the visit of Cardinal Pole to England, the Enniscorthy Friary joined with Kilcullen and other Franciscan houses in a petition seeking full restoration of their rights. At the time of the petition, complaint is made that the Friary at Enniscorthy was held without any title by Richard Butler.

In 1566 Nicholas Heron held the Friary grounds, and after 1575 Sir Richard Sinnott was the tenant. During short periods of relaxation in the religious persecution, the Friars occupied the Friary up to 1581. But the Elizabethan reign was a sorrowful epoch for the Enniscorthy Franciscans. During that long reign numerous grants and leases of the Friary are recorded to men with surnames like Briskett and Spenser, Stukely and Wallop.

CB

Thomas Stukely, an adventurer on the grand style, rented the property from Sir Richard Sinnott, whose tenancy is said to have been a nominal one. It is likely that Stukely lived for a time in the monastery building. In 1581 a lease of the Friary and castle was granted to Edmund Spenser, author of The Faery Queen. There is, however, no evidence that Spenser ever lived here; he went to reside on a large estate granted to him by Elizabeth at Kilcolman, Fermoy, Co. Cork.

In 1581 all the St John's property was granted to Lodowick Briskett, who was an intimate friend of Spenser. Briskett was an English poet of some distinction. He was the son of a Genoese father who had settled in England in 1535. When Sir Henry Sidney was appointed Lord Deputy for the third time in 1575, he brought Briskett to Ireland with him and had him appointed Clerk of the Privy Council. (Briskett's most famous poem was written on the death of Sir Philip Sidney.) After some time Briskett settled near Enniscorthy, holding much property, including St John's and Macmine, as well as Templescoby and Rossdroit. He also managed affairs in Enniscorthy for Sir Henry Wallop who got possession of both castle and Friary.

Sir Henry Wallop came to Ireland in 1579 as Treasurer of War for the Elizabethan administration. By 1585 he had got a firm grip of the Enniscorthy property; he reconstructed the castle and succeeded in amassing vast wealth for himself by cutting down the beautiful forests that stretched away to the north and west of the town. Wallop was well rewarded for his work in bringing this district once again under Government control. He was not yet satisfied and wrote several petitions seeking further rewards for his services. To quote his own words: "I presume I have deserved favour in greater measure for having planted at Enniscorthy, amongst so wild and barbarious a people."

Wallop's aims could be summarised as threefold — his own personal enrichment, the political conquest of Ireland and, something more important, the uprooting of the Catholic Faith, to which the people of County Wexford, both Gael and Norman, had shown such unshaken fidelity, even against the fiercest persecution. Wallop took a leading part in the events leading up to the torture and martyrdom of Dermot O'Hurley, Archbishop of Cashel. He actually signed the warrant for his execution.

Writing to Walsyngham in August, 1581, Wallop stated his view-point very succinctly: "There is no way to daunt these people but by the edge of the sword." In the following year, Fr Tadhg O Murchadha, Guardian of the Enniscorthy Friary, together with two of his community, his Vicar and sacristan, were seized by Wallop and a troop of soldiers, tortured for five days and hanged.

Wallop consolidated his position in Enniscorthy during the subsequent decade. We find an interesting entry in the Diary of the Lord Deputy, dated December 17, 1594: "Sir William Clark and Mr Briskett went to Enniscorthy to the Lady Wallop's for Christmas." They may have spent Christmas at the castle which Wallop had reconstructed, or perhaps at the Friary, for Wallop, we are informed, had turned part of the Friary building into a magnificent secular residence. He was firmly entrenched as master of this entire locality except for a temporary setback during the middle years of the Nine Years' War.

In 1597 the native Irish families here rose in alliance with Fiac Mac Hugh O'Byrne and with the two Hughs. Dónal Spáinneach Kavanagh threatened Wexford town and destroyed communication by the Slaney between Wexford and Enniscorthy. Briskett, in the course of a letter to Walsyngham in 1582, had boasted: "I am as well able to handle the sword as the pen." We can have no doubt as to his distinction as a poet, but it must be confessed there is little evidence of his prowess as a soldier when the testing time came. In April, 1598, the year in which the Battle of the Yellow Ford was fought, the royal forces suffered a disastrous defeat in a battle near Enniscorthy. The Kavanaghs attacked the town and Wallop's garrison was routed. Briskett collected what money and goods he could and fled with his wife and family to Waterford and took ship to England.

But the Irish triumph was short-lived. When the Tudor era came to an end in 1603, all Ireland had been forced into submission. The hopes raised by Hugh O'Neill's rebellion were dashed to the ground. The Franciscans in places like Enniscorthy could now only hope and pray for some favourable turn of events in the fortunes of Ireland.

In 1603 James I, son of Mary Stuart, became King of England. It was natural that the Irish Catholics should expect that the new king would not persecute the Faith for which his mother had died. In the principal cities of Ireland the churches were opened, the bells rang out, Mass was publicly celebrated, and Catholic ceremonies carried out with all the splendour of pre-Reformation times.

Then to the dismay of the Irish, Mountjoy sternly decreed that the public exercise of the Catholic religion could not be tolerated. Dr Grattan-Flood tell us that the Friars occupied the Enniscorthy monastery for a short spell at this time. When the persecution was resumed, they were forced to leave, but they continued to minister in disguise.

Fr Donagh Mooney, Provincial of the Irish Franciscans, visited Enniscorthy in 1617. His visit coincided in time with the preparations for the Plantation of North Wexford by Chichester. Fr Mooney's report is a most valuable document, containing very useful information not only on the Friary, but on the town generally.

He tells us that the monastery was founded by a certain Prince of Leinster, of the race of the Kavanaghs. The Friars did not live in their convent at the time of Fr Mooney's visit, but he tells us that there were people still living in the town who remembered seeing the Religious of the abbey scattered amongst their friends there, until with the passing of time they all died.

In the house of a certain nobleman, Fr Mooney was shown a chest in which was preserved a collection of Church vestments for the use of the Friary. Some of these sacred vestments were worked in gold, and they indicated clearly to Fr Mooney the piety and devotion of the people and the former splendour of the Church services at the Enniscorthy Friary. He goes on to tell how Sir Henry Wallop massacred the Friars and transformed part of the Friary building into a magnificent secular residence.

Fr Mooney, writing in Louvain in 1618, says that in spite of the persecution, "there are still 120 Franciscan friars in Ireland, and of these 35 are preachers who labour strenuously and with success; and there are 40 other Irish friars in Louvain preparing by prayer and study for work in Ireland."

The Franciscans returned to Enniscorthy in 1642, when the Confederation of Kilkenny was established after the success of the Rising of 1641. When the Friary was restored, Fr Richard Sinnot, OFM, was Guardian. He was sent there by the Provincial to undertake the task. He had five other Friars with him. The Confederation was formed in October, 1642, and in November of that year Fr Sinnot wrote from Enniscorthy to Fr Luke Wadding: "I am in a remote place. The Fr Provincial would have me come to Enniscorthy for the erection thereof and its settling. I am in it with five Friars besides myself. If I were able to maintain as many as do ask, and they get leave, I should have a great community." Fr Sinnot was succeeded as Guardian by Fr Bonaventure MacLoughlin, who was here till 1649.

The Franciscans were here when the Papal Nuncio to the Confederation, John Baptist Rinnuccini, visited Enniscorthy in 1647. He came to the town on a Sunday in April of that year and celebrated Mass here. In 1648 the Guardian closed the door of the Friary against a section of the Confederate army which had fallen under the Nuncio's censure. In May of the following year, Ormonde wrote a letter to Fr Redmond Carron, OFM, Franciscan Visitor to Ireland, accusing certain Irish members of the Order "of endeavouring to turn away the subjects from fidelity to the King and of disturbing the tranquillity of the Realm". The priests mentioned by Ormonde included Fr Bonaventure MacLoughlin, Guardian of Enniscorthy, and Fr James Sinnot, Guardian of Wexford.

ᛦ

This brings us to 1649 and the arrival of Oliver Cromwell in Ireland. His campaign heralded the dawn of a long period of dire suffering for the Catholic Church in Ireland, and the suppression of the Franciscan Houses. Let us quote Cromwell's own words describing his visit to Enniscorthy.

Writing to the Speaker of the English Parliament on October 14, 1649, Cromwell stated:

> "That night we marched into the fields of a village called Enniscorthy, belonging to Mr Robert Wallop, where was a strong castle, very well manned and provided for by the enemy, and close under it a very fair house belonging to the same worthy person, a monastery of Franciscan Friars, the considerablest in all Ireland; they ran away the night before we came."

Fr McLoughlin was Guardian when Cromwell came. We have already drawn attention to the fact that Cromwell spoke of the Enniscorthy Friary as "the considerablest in all Ireland"; his visit here was a tragic landmark in its history. The public work of the Franciscans in Enniscorthy was now ended, though it is related that for a long time afterwards they laboured in secret in the neighbourhood of the town. Readers will be familiar with the terrible events that followed Cromwell's campaign — the massacre at the Bull Ring and the murder of the Friars in Wexford, the sufferings endured by the bishop and priests of the diocese, the catastrophic fall in the population of the county; disease famine, pestilence, the vast land confiscations, and mass transportation.

One of the friars martyred for the Faith by Cromwell in Wexford was Fr Richard Sinnott, who was Guardian of Enniscorthy in 1642. He had become a Franciscan in

Portugal, and had occupied several important positions in the Order, including the Guardianship of the College of St Isidore's in Rome.

CB

Nowhere is the sad aftermath of Cromwell's onslaught seen so clearly as in the letters of the Bishop of this diocese, Dr Nicholas French, describing his own plight:

> "After the destruction of the town, I lived for five months in the woods … There my drink was milk and water, my food a little bread … I slept under the open sky without any shelter or covering. I wandered through wood and mountain, generally taking my rest exposed to the hoar frost, sometimes lying hidden in the caves and caverns of the earth."

At a Provincial Synod of the Irish Franciscans held at Ballydrohid, Laois, on September 23, 1651, Fr Dominic Dempsey, Guardian of Enniscorthy, was present. A rental of the Wallop estate in 1669 shows Morris Doyne as the tenant of "the House, Garden and Mill of Enniscorthy," at a yearly rent of £49. In his *Notes Towards A Parochial History of the Diocese of Ferns*, Dr W. H. Grattan Flood mentions that Philip Kelly was elected Guardian at the General Chapter held on September 8, 1661. In 1704, Fr Columba Kavanagh, OFM was Guardian. In 1743 John Wallop was made first Earl of Portsmouth.

Part of the Friary buildings lay in ruins. The history of the Franciscans in Enniscorthy during the seventeenth century is full at once of heroism and of pathos. They kept a long and faithful vigil before a feast that never came.

Even when their active ministrations had ceased, the Order continued to appoint titular Guardians of the Enniscorthy Convent until the middle of the nineteenth century. For the rest, the tale we have to tell is the story, not of the Friars, but of the Friary. "The ruined Friary kept silent watch by the Slaney for two centuries, a monument to the old faith of the town," wrote Fr Ranson in the *Cathedral Centenary Souvenir*.

There is a beautiful print of the Friary ruins in Sandby's Virtuosi's Museum, printed in 1778. This view had been reproduced in the Cathedral Centenary Souvenir. Paul Sandby was a painter and engraver, who made his paintings from sketches done on the spot. Reference is made to Sandby's paintings in a most interesting series of articles contributed by Fr Canice Mooney, OFM, in recent issues of the Journal of the Royal Society of Antiquaries of Ireland. His subject was Franciscan Architecture in Pre-Reformation Ireland. Sandby's book of paintings includes views of the Friaries at Adare, Askeaton and Carrig-on-Suir, as well as Enniscorthy.

"The most important of the paintings is that of Enniscorthy," writes Fr Mooney, "preserving for us as it does information that would otherwise have been lost about the friary of that town. It lay to the south of the town, beside the river Slaney, and on its west bank, with its garden running right down to the water's edge. The church was orientated and the domestic buildings lay to the north in the usual manner. The tower, following the regular Irish Franciscan pattern, was slender, tall, more or less square on plan, parapeted and placed at the intersection of nave and choir. In this view, however, it appears with a plain parapet, without battlements, and capped by a pyramidal roof, surmounted by a weather-vane."

The main entrance to the Friary building would have been the Castle Hill side, with the east window looking out towards the riverside.

ᙳ

Fr Canice Mooney alludes to the fact that the Enniscorthy Friary was known to the ancient annalists as Múr na mBráthar; the same title was given to the Abbey of Donegal. This brings to mind a quotation from the Irish poet's lament for another Franciscan Monastery, that of Timoleague:

A Mhúir naofa na mbeann nglas,
Dob órnaid don tir sea trath,
Is díomá dian liom do scrios
Agus cur do naomh ar fán.

Thomas Furlong (1794-1827), poet, of Scarawalsh, wrote a free translation of O Coileán's poem:

Here in soft strains the solemn
  Mass was sung;
Through these long aisles, the
  brethren bent their way;
Here the deep bell its wonted
  warning rung
to prompt the lukewarm, loitering
  one to pray.
Here the full choir sent forth its
  steam of sound
And the raised censer flung rich
  fragrance far around.

How changed the scene! How
  lonely now appears
The wasted aisle, wide arch and
  lofty wall,
The sculptured shape — the pride
  of other years,
Now darkened, shaded, sunk and
  broken all.

When Brewer, author of *The Beauties of Ireland*, visited Enniscorthy in 1825, he found part of the monastery building still in tolerable repair. "The remains of this friary stand on the river," he wrote, "and comprise a tower or steeple, together with the spacious kitchen, and the apartments of the

father guardian, which are in tolerable repair and inhabited".
We learn on the authority of George Griffiths that the
building was used as a hospital for sick soldiers in the second
half of the eighteenth century, and as a school between 1804
and 1826.

൦ൠ

Early in the last century great quantities of stones were
taken away when the outhouses had been dismantled.
Writing in 1835 Lewis tells us that "a great portion of the
conventual buildings have recently been removed in order to
furnish a site for the new market". He is referring to the
market shambles on the Abbey site, the erection of which
was commenced in 1832. The shambles project was
vigorously opposed by the vast majority of the traders of
Enniscorthy, who considered that it was yet another effort on
the part of Portsmouth, the town's absentee landlord, to
extract money from the townspeople by turning the Abbey
ground into a new source of revenue. The clearance of the
site for the erection of the shambles left the tower without
support. Lewis in 1836 says: "Of the Franciscan monastery,
the only remains are a lofty square tower on four pointed
arches" — nothing else was left.

൦ൠ

The tower collapsed in October, 1839. The famous Irish
scholar and antiquary, John O'Donovan, who visited
Enniscorthy in 1840, wrote: "The tower and other parts of the
monastery were in existence until about four months ago,
when they were blown down by a storm ... The site is
pointed out by the people on the bank of the river, very near
the castle. Part of the foundation of a wall, three or four feet
thick, which was a "portion of the old building, is still
traceable".

The exact date of the fall of the tower was October 23, 1839. The event was described in detail in a local newspaper, dated Wednesday, October 30 of that year. Here is the report:

> "The ancient and beautiful square tower belonging to the old Abbey, that for so many centuries ornamented the south-east side of Enniscorthy, and gave the landscape such a picturesque finish, particularly from the Wexford road, fell with a tremendous crash on the night of Wednesday last. Some time ago the buildings were taken away from about it to make room for improvements, and it was left supported only by the four pillars or jambs of the Gothic arches, and being thus unprotected from damp as well as storm, it is thought that during the excessive rain which fell on preceding days, it imbibed so much wet that the mortar losts its bond, and in a sudden gust, it was overbalanced and in an instant became a heap of stones."

ଓଃ

A beautiful stone doorway preserved in the premises of Messrs G. H. Lett was formerly part of the Friary building, according to a very reliable local tradition. When the tower fell, and the debris was being cleared, a gold brooch, enriched with emeralds and garnets, was found. It is preserved in the British Museum and is called the Enniscorthy Friary Brooch.

In 1839, after the fall of the tower, the Bishop of Ferns, Dr Keating, had large quantities of stones removed from the ruins of the Friary to the grounds of the old thatched Cathedral. These stones were used in the building of the new Cathedral on the same site.

At the Abbey grounds not a single vestige of the Franciscan Friary now survives. Only the place-names — Abbey Square, Friary Hill, Friary Place — remain to remind us of its ancient glory. The stones of the old Friary are to be seen in the walls of the modern Cathedral. Pugin's Church, built by Dr Keating in the middle of the nineteenth century, is in fact the only memorial that exists to the Franciscan Abbey founded by Dónal Reagh in the fifteenth century.

ᛣ

ENNISCORTHY'S GREAT REPEAL MEETING*

*Appeared in The Echo, July 1963, after the visit of President Kennedy to Co. Wexford.

The visit of President Kennedy to his ancestral home in County Wexford last month brought wonderful enthusiastic gatherings and an upsurge of national and local pride seldom equalled in our recent history. The demonstrations of spontaneous, popular feeling recall to mind another great concourse of Wexfordmen, which heralded the awakening of true national spirit, though in less happy circumstances. I refer to the famous Repeal meeting addressed by Daniel O'Connell in Enniscorthy in July, 1843, exactly 120 years ago this month.

∞

The Liberator was then at the zenith of his popularity and power. The Enniscorthy meeting was held in the place near "Red Pat's Cross" still called "The Repeal Field", and ranks with the Hill of Tara gathering as one of the largest of the Repeal Monster meetings.

The weekly newspaper of the Young Ireland movement, *The Nation*, founded in 1842 by Thomas Davis, Charles Gavan Duffy and John Blake Dillon, described the Enniscorthy meeting in these words:

> "Ireland has reason to be proud of Wexford. Wexford has good right to be proud of itself; and though the

meetings that have taken place in other counties were characterised by all the ennobling traits of patriotic ardour, they were nothing superior to the really glorious outburst of popular feeling which marked the proceedings of to-day. The history of Ireland makes honourable mention of the struggle made by the men of Wexford at every period when the principles of civil and religious freedom were to be advanced, and the same record of past events proclaims the warm and underrating patriotism of their ancestors who in less fortunate times, fought under less auspicious circumstances."

There is a striking resemblance between the sentiments expressed in this paragraph and the sentences spoken by President Kennedy at New Ross:

"When my great-grandfather left the port of New Ross to become a cooper in East Boston, he carried nothing with him except two things — a strong religious faith and a great desire for liberty. I am glad to say that all his grandchildren have valued that inheritance."

The Enniscorthy meeting took place on a Thursday. Daniel O'Connell left Dublin on Wednesday morning and reached Arklow at two o'clock in the afternoon, where crowds of people flocked round his carriage and applauded him enthusiastically. All along the road he received the same welcome. At Gorey, hundreds of horsemen met him and great crowds cheered him. At Camolin he was met by V. Rev. Edward Kavanagh, parish priest of Ballyoughter and Camolin, and his parishioners. He was accompanied to Ferns by hundreds of people, led by V. Rev. Fr Roche, parish priest of Ferns, and his two curates, Fr Meyler and Fr Brownrigg. Here he was welcomed by over 600 horsemen from Enniscorthy. The cheering along the road was immense, and "The Liberator" acknowledged the congratulations of the people. At seven o'clock he arrived at Summerhill, the residence of Most Rev. Dr Keating, Bishop of Ferns, where he attended a dinner party.

Dr Keating had been Consecrated Bishop in 1819. He was the man responsible for the erection of St Aidan's Cathedral; in fact work on the new cathedral was commencing at the date when the Repeal meeting took place. The bishop was a strong supporter and personal friend of Daniel O'Connell. When on one occasion O'Connell was imprisoned in Dublin, Dr Keating visited him in prison. When O'Connell died at Genoa on his way to Rome in May, 1847, the Bishop of Ferns was one of the prelates present at Dun Laoghaire to receive his remains.

From an early hour on the Thursday morning huge crowds from all over the county were gathering into the town of Enniscorthy. No fewer than 150 boat-loads of people arrived by the Slaney from Wexford to attend the Repeal demonstration. *The Nation* wrote:

> "The people of Forth and Bargy, joined by the trades and inhabitants of Wexford, proceeded along the Edermine road with bands playing and colours flying, to where the procession was formed. Large masses from Taghmon, Gorey, Ferns, Oulart, Ballygarret, Kilmuckridge, Kilcormack, Blackwater, Newtonbarry, Kilmyshall, Shambo, Ross, Tomacork, Clonegal, Carnew, Kildavin came into town this morning headed by their bands playing appropriate airs. At ten o'clock the trades of Enniscorthy assembled near the Castle, and they proceeded to the bishop's residence, where they presented an address to O'Connell, to which he returned a suitable reply."

The procession was then joined by "the Liberator" and proceeded on its route from Summerhill by the Presentation Convent, Duffry Gate, by the Cathedral, Main Street, Rafter Street (then Back Street) and along the newly-built road from the Millpark to St John's Bridge, thence to the field at Tomduff.

Some of the newspapers recorded the mottoes written on the banners of the various trades in the procession, like smith, slaters, masons. The motto of the carpenters was, "Unity is strength — the sons of St Joseph"; the tailors, "I was naked and you clothed me". The motto of the labourers was, "Welcome, Ireland's Liberator — Labour, Employment and Wages — Peace and Plenty". On one side of the weaver's banner was a representation of a round tower, a wolf dog and a harp, with the motto, "Ireland as she was"; on the other side a representation of a woolpack, a wheel and a weaver at work, with the motto, "Ireland as she will be".

At eleven o'clock arrived the veteran and illustrious Thomas Cloney at the head of thousands of men from Carlow and Kilkenny to swell the vast throng. His coming stirred heroic memories of the fight at the Three Rocks and the exploits of the Bantrymen and the Battle of Ross. Observers estimated the attendance at several hundred thousand people; there were tens of thousands waiting for hours in the Repeal Field before the Liberator's procession arrived. Tradition says that thousands of people travelled on foot 30 or 40 miles to the meeting.

The platform party included many distinguished figures, priests and laity. Amongst these was Fr Hore, PP, Tinahely; Fr Walsh, PP, Kilmore; Fr Pettit, PP, Oylegate; Fr Stafford, PP, Ballygarret; Fr Cullen, PP, Rathangan; Fr Furlong Screen; Gen. Thomas Cloney; Thomas Francis Meagher and Alderman Delahunty from Waterford; R. Smithwick, Kilkenny; Tom Steele, Dublin; E. Hay and T. Houlett, New Ross.

Prominent Enniscorthy men mentioned were John Hore of The Moyne, who gave evidence on behalf of the tenant-farmers before the Devon Commission in the same year, and Patrick White, who had been imprisoned for his part in the struggle against the tithes.

Opening the meeting, Dr Keating, Bishop of Ferns, said:

> "My dear friends of the County Wexford, you have come here quiet, orderly, peaceable, moral men, such

as you always have been, for that is your character. The Legislative Union between Great Britain and Ireland has reduced us to a poor, pitiful and pelted province. It has struck down our trade and commerce, and has ruined our manufactures. Is Ireland to remain in vassalage and in bondage?" (Cheers and shouts of "Never!").

"In this momentous and great undertaking — to restore to Ireland her domestic Parliament — you have the first man in Europe to assist you, 'the Liberator', whose name will be handed down to the latest posterity, the man of a thousand battles and a thousand victories, all bloodless. Let us pledge ourselves, one and all, never to abandon that sacred and holy cause until we shall see Ireland as she ought to be —

> *Great, glorious and free,*
> *First flower of the earth, first*
> *gem of the sea."*

Dr Keating then introduced the Chairman of the meeting, John Maher of Ballinkeele, who opened his speech with three well-known lines from Walter Scott:

> *Breathes there a man with soul*
> *so dead,*
> *Who never to himself hath said,*
> *'This is my own, my native*
> *land?'*

A series of resolutions in support of Repeal was then put to the meeting and short speeches delivered by Rev. Dr Sinnot, President of St Peter's College; John Hyacinth Talbot; Sheppard Jeffries, Mayor of Wexford; Victor O'Ferrall, Ballyanne; John T. Devereux, Wexford; Edmund Stafford,

Ballymore; W. B. Cooke, Court; Clement Roice, Churchtown; T. Meyler, Harristown, and G. Downes, Adamstown.

Mr Cooke in his address said that the loyalist Press was certain to convey to Sir Robert Peel the story of that great meeting for Repeal — 300,000 men assembled within view of the classic ground of Vinegar Hill.

Loud, prolonged applause greeted Daniel O'Connell when he rose to deliver his speech. "It has been my good fortune to have witnessed large masses of my countrymen," he declared, "but I never saw so noble an assembly as the present. It exceeds in magnitude any that I have ever addressed before".

His address was a typical O'Connell oration, rich in powerful eloquence couched in homely language, rousing rather than persuasive, full of shafts of wit and sarcasm and humorous attacks upon his adversaries. Each brief argument was rounded off with a series of rhetorical questions to his vast audience, which drew forth frequent rounds of applause, alternating with peals of laughter.

He assured his audience of the certainty of the success of the Repeal movement. "Our enemies have exhausted all their threats," he said. "The fellow that stood above Enniscorthy Bridge waiting till the Slaney had passed by that he might walk over dryshod was a wise fellow compared with the Duke of Wellington who thinks that he has only to stand by a little and that the Irish will give up the pursuit of that freedom which is their right and which they will never relax their efforts to obtain until the Parliament is in College Green. (Cheers and laughter).

"I despise the man who even for wealth would consent to be a slave. Repeal is on the wild winds of Heaven. The breeze fresh from Wexford is flowing over it; that gale is scattering through Ireland. The seeds of Liberty are upon the pinions of that wind and they shall cover the entire land with the angel wing of protection and freedom."

He referred to the exploits of the Duke of Wellington at
the Battle of Waterloo and added:

> "If he was not a better general than he is a logician, he
> would be the greatest dunderhead that every yet was
> at the head of an army." (Cheers). "From the first time
> the English placed a hostile foot on the green soil of
> Wexford, they never defeated us in battle by fair and
> open fight. They never gained any advantage over us
> but by deceiving and cheating us."

He then restated, amidst loud applause, the unanswerable
argument against tithes, and proceeded to criticise both the
Grand Jury Cess and the poor rate. He went on to deal with
the Land Question. Though he criticised the landlords in a
mild way, the changes he asked for would be considered far
too moderate by the later advocates of land reform like
Gavan Duffy in 1851 or Michael Davitt in 1881.

> "There is another and greater evil still felt in other
> counties and, of course, in this, it is the horrible
> clearance system of turning out tenants. I want a fixity
> of tenure; I want that no tenure shall be less than 21
> years, no rent recoverable except upon a lease of 21
> years, no lease, no rent." (Cheers). "I believe these
> things would be good."

"Three hundred years of persecution rolled over you," he
said, as he told the story of the Penal Laws. He dealt in detail
with the massacre in the Bull ring in 1649:

> "I never went through the Bull Ring of Wexford that I
> did not send up a petition to Providence that one day
> Ireland would have retribution, not in blood but in
> mercy from Heaven for that cruelty.
>
> "The morning of Liberty is coming upon us;
> Liberty shall be re-echoed from our mountain rocks
> and the young eagle of Irish freedom shall soar aloft
> proclaiming to the congregated world that it was by

virtuous men and virtuous men alone, that Ireland
rose to legislative independence. Yes, our country
shall be free."

After the meeting the great procession was reformed and
marched back to Summerhill by Millpark Road, Slaney Place,
Island road and Bohreen Hill. The Government drafted large
numbers of troops into Enniscorthy to watch the
proceedings. *The Nation's* comment was:

"There were large bodies of cavalry and infantry in
town, but it is unnecessary to add that they were not
required. In fact, it was a burlesque to have them
there."

A banquet took place in the evening in a pavilion a
hundred feet long erected for the occasion. A thousand
people attended this banquet, and we are told that
"chandeliers of very exquisite construction were suspended
from the ceiling". In a short address, the Liberator said:

"My mind is filled with the majestic scene that
appeared before me at to-day's meeting. I see what a
quantity there is here of physical force, of moral
power — what a quantity of intellect of physical
energy — all those elements that elevate nations from
prostrate situations and raise them to the station of
independence and power. I am going round on my
circuit. On Sunday next I shall be with John of Tuam."
(Cheers). "On Sunday week I shall be in Castlebar,
and on August 15, I shall be on the Hill of Tara."

 CB

A STRONG BRAVE BRIDGE*

*This appeared in The Echo on 27 November 1965 after serious floods in Enniscorthy.

I have been requested to write a short article on the two bridges that span the Slaney at Enniscorthy, bridges which have figured so much in the news due to the disastrous floods of last week.

The Railway Bridge is a hundred and one years old. The first train ever to come to Enniscorthy arrived on November 16, 1863. Shortly after this date, work commenced on the building of the new Railway Bridge. On October 15, 1864, the *Enniscorthy News* reported:

> "In a few days the abutments of the new bridge will be so much above the water that no ordinary 'fresh' in the river will interrupt the work."

Within a few months, the work on the Railway Bridge was completed and the building of the tunnel commenced. The same newspaper then for the first time broke the news to the citizens of Enniscorthy that the new tunnel "is to start at Mary Street and end near the Model School".

If the Railway Bridge was damaged last week, we can say in all fair play that "no ordinary 'fresh' in the river" did damage.

ENNISCORTHY BRIDGE

The road bridge over the Slaney dates from 1680. Although it is quite true that in the Elizabethan era an elaborate plan for a bridge here was designed by a man called Paul Finglas, the idea never materialised.

Robert Leigh, Rosegarland, writing in 1684, referred to Enniscorthy "where a large stone bridge is lately built".

In 1682, Solomon Richards, in his account of the town, wrote that Enniscorthy Bridge had been built two years previously. In 1837 the bridge was lowered and widened. The task was carried out jointly by the Grand Jury of the county and the trustees of the Portsmouth Estate. At that period, the Portsmouth Estate took some interest in the welfare of the town.

When Sir William Brereton visited Enniscorthy on his way to Wexford in 1835, he crossed the river on horseback because there was no bridge.

"We went towards Wexford,"

he says in his diary,

"which is accounted eight miles, but they are very long miles. We crossed the water at Enniscorthy on horseback and at the Carrick, a mile from Wexford, we passed over a narrow ferry."

Numerous visitors to the town have spoken in admiration of the beauty and gracefulness of Enniscorthy Bridge. I distinctly remember the late Mr Richard Hayward, the Belfast historian, praise with enthusiasm the stonework of the bridge. Just as the old Wexford Bridge is associated in the minds of the people with Harvey, Grogan and Matthew Keogh, so Enniscorthy Bridge is linked with the names William Barker and Father Mogue Kearns, who fought gailantly at this very spot on June 21, 1798, the day that General Lake opened his assault on Vinegar Hill.

When in 1682 Solomon Richards mentioned the bridge, he described it as "a strong, brave bridge," a description that now seems very apt, seeing that it withstood so gallantly the uncontrollable torrent of last week.

ISLAND STRAND

In many of the old maps the Island Road was called "Island Strand", a title which bears a certain significance when considered in the context of last week's conditions. In the same way as "The Night of the Big Wind" in 1839 lived on in the minds of the people for several generations, so will the floods of last week be remembered. People in coming generations will speak of November 1965, as the "Time of the Big Floods". People will remember also that the need to meet this great crisis sparked off a wonderful community effort, magnificent in its spontaneity and unequalled in the long history of the town.

SCARAWALSH BRIDGE

Postscript — While dealing with the subject of bridges, a brief reference to the Scarawalsh Bridge will not be out of place.

On this point I have found a useful quotation in one of my notebooks which is worth reproducing. It is a letter dated 1790 (in the month of November):

> "From Ferns I rode to Scarawalsh, where the masons were building an elegant bridge over the beautiful River Slaney, the old one having been swept away by the inundation in 1787, and then proceeded by the side of the river to Enniscorthy, passing near Solsborough, the seat of Solomon Richards, Esq. Enniscorthy is a handsome town pleasantly situated on each side of the River Slaney, and joined by a large stone bridge."

[The original source of this is a description of County Wexford by a Traveller in Walker's *Hibernian Magazine*.]

೮೫

COOLAMAIN BLEACH GREEN

The story of flax-growing and linen manufacture in this county over the centuries is a chapter of Wexford's industrial history which has never been written. At no period could it be claimed that Wexford was ever amongst the leading linen counties of Ireland, yet flax-culture and linen-making were so widely carried on in all parts of Wexford as to give them a significant place amongst the occupations of the rural community.

When Arthur Young travelled through County Wexford in 1776 he found that in the district around Courtown "a little flax is sown, generally after potatoes, and the culture of it increases gradually". Earlier in the same century, the Colcloughs (the name is pronounced "Coakley") had established at Tintern a spinning school and linen factory. The Carew Papers and Account Books frequently contain entries on local linen-making in the Castleboro area. For instance, in 1771 we find these entries: "To weaving 42 yards diaper at 7d. per yard," and "To bleaching 32 yards of linen at 2d. per yard". Again in 1773 it was recorded, "To a weaver for weaving 38 yards diaper at 1s. per yard" and on May 29 of same year, "For bleaching 38 yards of diaper at 2d. per yard". (Diaper was an unbleached linen cloth, woven in slightly ornamental pattern, used for towels).

Shaw-Mason's Parochial Survey of Ireland (1814) mentions linen in several parishes in the county; writing of Whitechurch, New Ross, he says, "Peas and flax are occasionally grown, but not for sale". About the same time, a very observant writer, John Bernard Trotter, travelling through the north of the county, saw crops of flax in a very good state between Coolgreaney and Camolin. "The linen manufacture," he says, "has made respectable but not great progress in Wexford." Describing his journey from Bunclody to Ross, he wrote, "Flax is a good deal but not sufficiently introduced and seldom more than a quarter of an acre of flax in a farm is cultivated. There is, nevertheless, a little everywhere".

The local correspondent who contributed the information from Tintern parish to Mason's Parochial Survey, wrote:

> "The only manufactures carried on are those of linens and woollens; with the former little is done, except for home consumption, though we have some remarkably good diaper weavers, and the parish is well adapted for the linen business, as flax grows well and is already cultivated to some extent."

When the four Union workhouses were established in the county under the Poor Law Act of 1838, the newly formed Boards of Guardians set the inmates working at the manufacture of linens. In September, 1844, the Enniscorthy Guardians accepted a tender from a man named Lacy "to keep the spinning wheels in order for six months at 1s. 6d. each". Tenders for the supply of dressed flax were frequently accepted, and mention is made of the weaver's shop. In 1852 one of the Guardians reported, "In the girls' school there are over 40 flax wheels at work and the thread made by the children is of excellent quality". When the inspector arrived from the National Board he complained that "the spinning wheels occupy so much space that the girls are too crowded. Those learning writing and arithmetic have not sufficient room at their desks". In the same year, John Maher of Ballinkeele, a leading member of the Board of Guardians had a sample of dressed flax exhibited to the board, prepared from flax grown on the workhouse grounds, 19 lb. weight from one cwt. of flax straw; the flax was of very superior quality.

It should be emphasised that linen manufacture in Wexford, even when in its state of healthiest vigour, was essentially a domestic industry, which the rural community used to supplement their earnings from the land. The introduction of new and improved methods in both spinning and weaving lead to the disappearance of this domestic industry in places like Wexford and to the ultimate localisation of the linen trade in the province of Ulster.

The domestic nature of the industry is clearly evident from sources like Lewis' Topographical Dictionary; speaking of Carne parish, he says, "Some coarse linen and linsey-wolsey are manufactured here for home consumption," and referring to Donaghmore, he observes, "A domestic manufacture of strong linen is carried on here, in which nearly all the female cottagers are employed".

There is abundant evidence to show that linen was of considerable importance in the rural economy. Many Wexford families still preserve pieces of linen made in the county from flax grown on local farms. In the written records there is frequent mention of flax mills, while the memory of the old-time linen trade survives in local tradition − the growing of flax, the crafts of spinning and weaving, the itinerant weavers, the location of bleaching greens in various parts of the county.

The Bleach Green of Coolamain (Oylegate) was one of the most important centres of its kind in Wexford. It was established by the Atkins family in 1736, and there are very frequent references to it in local records for over a century.

The Atkins family held the property from the local landlord, Arthur Gore, and the lease was renewed "under the Act of Parliament giving power to certain persons of making leases of land for the purpose of building and carrying on the linen manufacture". When the lease was renewed in 1809, the proprietor is described a "William Atkin, of Coolamain, Bleacher," and the property is referred to as "that part of the town and lands of Coolamain commonly called The Bleach, on which a house, offices and mill have been erected". The land contained almost eleven acres, Plantation measure, at a yearly rent of £22 3s.

But in this instance the tenant had to pay an annual rent for the water as well as for the land. On September 19, 1785,

William Atkin leased the stream by the river Sow from Mathew Talbot of Castle Talbot for 21 years at an annual rent of £2 5s. 6d. The actual wording was as follows:

> "All that stream or piece of water then and for many years past in the occupation of the said William Atkins, commonly called or known by the name of The Head Weir running to the Bleach Green and Corn Mill of Coolamain."

In the Wexford Herald, dated May 9, 1809, William Atkins published an advertisement informing his friends and the general public that his "Bleach Green in Coolamain is now open for the reception of linens, where the usual care and attention will be taken to have them well-finished, and safe, as he will make ample satisfaction for any piece damaged". Linens were taken in at three places named in the advertisement — at the Bleach Green, at the office of Christopher Taylor, printer, Main Street, Wexford, proprietor of the Wexford Herald, and at the shop of Richard Freeman, clock-maker, Enniscorthy.

At the same time, the proprietor of the Taghmon Bleach Green published an advertisement on similar lines, promising that "a compensation of five shillings per yard will be paid for every yard of linen that may be damaged in bleaching". Linens were accepted on his behalf at named shops in Wexford, Ross and Enniscorthy; at John Scallan's of Tagoat, John Howlin's of Kilmore, Miles Kinsella's of Bridgetown, and John Breen's of Taghmon.

Twenty years later, John and Mary Atkins were the proprietors of the Coolamain Bleach Green. In an advertisement printed in the Wexford Herald on May 14, 1828, they offered thanks to the public for continued patronage and they hoped "by care and attention to merit a continuance of that kind patronage they have always experienced".

In 1845 the Bleach Green was in the hands of Joseph Kehoe. In May of that year, the clerk of Enniscorthy Union

Guardians was directed to get tenders from three Bleach Greens — Mullinderry, Coolamain and Shillelagh "for the bleaching of about seven hundred yards of the linen, woven from the threads, manufactured in the house, and now ready for that process". It is recorded that the tender of Joseph Kehoe of Coolamain was accepted, to bleach the linen, giving it a quarter bleach, for a sum of one penny per yard.

After the Insurrection of 1798 hundreds of claims were made to the Government for compensation for damage done to property during the course of the Rising. One of these claims was from Wm. Atkin of Coolamain for £478 13s. 8d. for loss of linens and other articles, but primarily for the "Loss of the Bleaching Season" in that year. 1798 was a warm, dry summer. Wm. Atkin's application was not granted.

The Bleach Green is clearly marked on the early Ordinance Survey maps; though always described as the Coolamain Bleach Green, it was actually situated within the bounds of the modern townland called Bleachlands, on the banks of the Sow River. The district was within the old parish of Ballinaslaney, part of which was in the Barony of Shelmalier and part in the Barony of Ballaghkeene.

In the valuation records for 1844 Edward Kehoe was the owner of the Bleach Green and Flat Mill, while the corn mill of Mill Lands was jointly held by John Atkins and Edward Kehoe.

A surveyor's report on Edward Kehoe's flax mill tells us that it was in operation for six months in each year. It contained an engine for finishing the linens. "The water wheel is a small one about nine feet in diameter and two feet in breadth," he says. The dimensions of the mill itself were 16½ feet long, 16 feet broad and 12 feet high.

A Bleach Green of considerable importance was that of Owenduff in the Barony of Shelburne. In the years after 1798 there are numerous references to it and as late as 1837 Samuel Lewis observes:

"A stream called the Awenduffe or Blackwater is tributary to the Barrow river, and separates the baronies of Shelburne and Shelmalier. At Yoletown are two flour-mills, worked by the Blackwater, and there are also two bleachgreens on the banks of that river."

A directory of 1824 says:

"The principle trade that is carried on in Enniscorthy is in corn, and next to Clonmel this is considered the greatest inland corn market in Ireland."

Ten years later Inglis visited the town, and on the day of his arrival "there was a brisk corn market and a large number of people in the streets, buying and selling".

The principal corn market was in the Irish Street. Inglis added: "The corn of the greater part of the county of Wexford passes through the market of Enniscorthy and is shipped there." There is ample evidence to show that the greater part of this corn trade was in barley.

∞

Students of Irish economic history are familiar with the quotation that the prosperity of Cork was built upon butter. With equal truth it could be asserted that the prosperity of Enniscorthy was built upon barley. In 1796 there were no less than 23 registered malt-houses in the town. 40 years later the number was much higher. From a report dated 1836 we find that annually there were 60,000 tons of grain sent down by boat on the Slaney from Enniscorthy to Wexford.

Two points may be mentioned here as clearly indicative of the change-over to the barley economy. The foundry site on the present premises of Lett's about 1810 became a mill, malt-house and brewery, while a decade later Andrew Jameson purchased for use as a distillery the old Ironworks at Fairfield. In the 1830s there was a distillery on part of the site now occupied by Roche's maltings.

In the last half of the nineteenth century returns were issued indicating the fluctuations in the acreage under various crops in Wexford county; the area under corn declined sharply following the repeal of the Corn Laws, but it is a significant fact that the acreage under barley declined less than the other forms of grain.

Yet the halcyon days of the corn trade had gone; for this and other reasons the population declined. According to the Census of 1861 the quality of many of the dwellings in the town left much to be desired.

ର

The fifth and final phase in Enniscorthy's expansion took place during the present century. By 1900 the era of private house-building had passed; the responsibility for providing houses now fell on the local authorities. Enniscorthy's first Urban Council was elected in 1899 and in a short time it erected a row of houses at Patrick's Street. A further scheme was carried out a few years later at Patrick's Place and Lower Shannon. Before World War I, houses were erected by the Council at Upper Shannon, Redmond Street and Ross Road.

There is no need to describe here the bigger schemes undertaken by the Council in recent years, the first of which was St John's Villas, completed in 1931, and the last of which was Bellefield Road and Fr Cullen Terrace. The Council built in all over 600 houses. These were well-planned and provided with better amenities; they were erected for the most part in spacious streets on the level ground beyond the steep slope from the riverside.

Enniscorthy has grown slowly out of the centuries. The Shannon had its origin in an ecclesiastical foundation, while it was for military reasons the Castle was built. The growth of the remaining streets is more closely related to economic factors. This variety of origin has led to a certain haphazardness in its development which is one of the features often admired by visitors.

Amidst this loud chorus of praise we should not overlook the town's shortcomings — its very steepness has hampered physical expansion. Amongst the towns of Ireland it has been, and still is, noted for its high density of population, a large number of people concentrated inside too small an area.

CB

Employment in the town over the centuries has seldom been able to keep pace with the size of the population. The *Parliamentary Gazetteer* of 1846 remarked:

> "Enniscorthy Town is singularly irregular ... Its streets have two or three plots of spaciousness but in general are nearly as remarkable for their narrowness as for their irregularity and capricious crookedness."

But, strangely enough, it is this very irregularity which gives Enniscorthy much of its colour and charm. The same writer goes on to add:

> "The streets are edificed in such a fashion as to give the town an ancient and half-Oriental appearance."

Other towns of more modern origin can boast a greater regularity. They are excellently planned, but it is this excess of order which mars their appearance. The visitor is appalled by the prevailing dullness arising from a sickening surfeit of symmetry.

Many visitors have referred to the delightful wooded approach to Enniscorthy from the north. If I may add a personal note — how many towns can boast anything so wonderful as "the Island" — Patrick Kennedy in 1819 referred to it as "the flat green Island above the Bridge" — that magnificent green expanse so near the heart of the town, stretching from the Railway Bridge to "the Sally Tree".

A feature of Enniscorthy's streets which merits mention is the colourful shop fronts and artistically-painted signs which have so frequently won the admiration of visitors.

Recent years have seen the awakening amongst the people of a greater feeling of pride, a growing sense of good citizenship, a desire to co-operate with the local authority in preserving the native beauty of the town, to make it less unworthy of the praise lavished on it by writers like Aodh de Blacam:

> "If it were in France or Italy, the world would hear of Enniscorthy's beauty; painters and etchers would depict it in a hundred aspects."

ꝏ

THE COMING OF THE RAILWAY*

*Appeared in The Echo, *July 1962*

The first railway built in Ireland was the line from Dublin to Dun Laoghaire. That was in 1834. Gradually the line was extended southwards, though the work was interrupted by the Famine of 1846-7. A hundred years ago this month, in July, 1862 the Dublin line reached into County Wexford for the first time. On July 11, 1862, a contract was signed to extend the railway from Arklow as far as Enniscorthy. The cost was £73,000 or approximately £2,500 a mile.

The railway was laid down through Inch, Gorey, Camolin, Ferns, and on Monday, November 16, 1863, the first train ever to steam into Enniscorthy's newly-built station arrived. The train came at 12 noon amidst scenes of great public excitement. It was a fair day in the town, and crowds thronged the platform all day. In honour of the occasion a band paraded the streets, and in the evening there was a display of fireworks on the Island.

Work commenced shortly afterwards on the new railway bridge over the Slaney. On October 15, 1864, a local newspaper reported: "In a few days' time the abutments will be so much above the water that no ordinary 'fresh' in the river will interrupt the work." By that time preparations for building the new tunnel under the town had begun; we are told that it was "to start at Mary Street and end near the Model School". The railway intersected Mary Street, which was on the old coach route between Dublin and Wexford, and led to the building of the Railway Hill. A special meeting of the Town Commissioners petitioned the Board of Trade to reduce the gradient of the new hill.

The construction of the railway between Rathdrum and Enniscorthy, a distance of over 40 miles, was finished in two years. It took nine years to build the line from Enniscorthy to Wexford. Main cause of the delay was, of course, the Tunnel, a task which made the railway work costly as well as slow. All this could have been avoided had the original intention been carried out by bringing the line from the present station along Templeshannon Quay, cutting a path for it parallel to the present Wexford Road, and crossing the river some distance below the town. But this proposal was strenuously opposed by the leading merchants of Enniscorthy. They cherished the hope that a wonderful future was in store for the town if the Slaney river traffic could be properly developed, perhaps by the building of a canal.

Throughout the entire century this idea was frequently mentioned. At one time it was proposed to build a canal between Pouldarrig and Brownswood. A railway bridge over the Slaney anywhere below the town would end this dream of a great river canal. It is difficult to believe that the objection of these citizens was the fruit of a robust faith in river transport, for the coming of the railway — whatever course it took — was bound ultimately to lead to the decline of the Slaney as a channel of commerce.

Their viewpoint was rather the expression of a wistful hope. Yet it led to the building of the Tunnel, an engineering feat of considerable magnitude. Work was commenced simultaneously at both ends, and a very large number of men were employed. Week by week the *Enniscorthy News* reported on the progress of the Tunnel — February 18, 1865:

> "The Tunnel under the town has been commenced at the rear of Mr O'Dempsey's house in Slaney Street, and is making satisfactory progress."

April 7, 1866:

> "On Tuesday night last, about 10 o'clock, the men working at the above tunnel met about midway. So

now any person entering it at one end can pass through."

For many years Enniscorthy remained the terminus of the Dublin railway line. When Cardinal Cullen came on his official visit to Wexford in 1869, he travelled from Dublin to Enniscorthy by rail, and completed his journey by road carriage to Wexford. The building of the Tunnel at Ferrycarrig was a difficult and slow task. The railway between Macmine and Ballywilliam was opened before the line between Enniscorthy and Wexford was finished. In its issue of October 8, 1870, *The Watchman* (Enniscorthy) reported:

"The works on this railway are being carried on with great spirit and rapidity, nearly 500 men and 30 horses being employed on the line. Three miles are finished to foundation level, one to level of sleepers. The tunnels at The Deeps and Ferrycarrig have been excavated to the length of 36 and 44 yards, respectively, the lining of 33 yards of the latter being finished. The masonry of the thirteen bridges is complete."

The first passenger train reached Wexford on August 17, 1872. Ten years later the line was extended to Ballygeary (now Rosslare). The landing pier was then incomplete, the Cross-channel service to Fishguard was not inaugurated till two further decades has passed. It was originally proposed to link the Rosslare line with Waterford by building a bridge over the river at Ballyhack, but the proposal was abandoned in favour of the present line through Wellington Bridge and Campile, crossing the river at a point below Checkpoint. Following objections by New Ross Harbour Commissioners, a Parliamentary enquiry endorsed the new proposals but special by-laws had to be made to facilitate shipping to and from New Ross. The link with Waterford opened up Rosslare to the southern counties of Ireland.

The line was originally called the Dublin, Wicklow and Wexford Railway. Sir James Power of Edermine was a director. In 1888 it was extended to New Ross by continuing the line already constructed from Macmine. A further extension was made in 1904 to link this railway with Waterford, and so the local network was completed. The name of the company was then changed to Dublin and South-Eastern Railways (DSER). When the railways were amalgamated in 1925 by an Act passed by Dáil Eireann, the DSER merged into the Great Southern Railway (GSR), later nationalised and called Córas Iompair Eireann.

The Second Report of the Railway Commissioners in 1835 is a valuable source of local history and is, in fact, an economic survey of the areas covered by the proposed railway network. All the early plans included a junction on the main line at Scarawalsh linking through the Slaney Valley with Bunclody and Tullow and penetrating into County Carlow. This extension never materialised, although at one stage notices were actually served on the owners and occupiers of land. If this idea of a junction at Scarawalsh had been carried out, the path of the railway would have run on the western outskirts of Enniscorthy, and hence there would have been no need for the building of the Tunnel.

ষ্টেও

Apart from matters like the building of new roadways and rail sidings, and the partial dislocation of water supplies, the coming of the railway had a far-reaching effect on the economic life of Enniscorthy. It enhanced the importance of the town as a centre of industry and trade. It led to the decline of the extensive Slaney river traffic, and the coastal shipping between Wexford and Dublin. For generations there had been a considerable trade from Enniscorthy in the inland carriage of agricultural produce to Dublin. The railway brought this traffic to an end. It led to the decay of many of the old crafts and house industries, and contributed ultimately to the creation of larger units of production in industries like malting and milling, and to the disappearance of others like textiles and tanning. On the other hand, the railway helped to increase the importance of the town's fairs and markets and, not of least significance, made it easier for Enniscorthy to exploit its natural advantages as a centre of distribution.

ೞ

ENNISCORTHY'S FIRST FIRE BRIGADE

The first Fire Service ever established in Enniscorthy dates back as far as 1707. The Corporation of the borough in that year set up an effective system of night-watching to prevent fires, a fact which has attracted the attention of historians, because it was singular amongst provincial towns in Ireland at that time.

In the town records there is frequent mention of serious fires in Enniscorthy throughout the eighteenth century, at a time when most of the houses were thatched. The most extensive fire record was in 1731. On March 15 of that year Urban's *Gentlemen's Magazine* reported:

> "A dreadful fire broke out in the town of Enniscorthy and consumed 42 dwellinghouses there."

Smaller fires occurred in 1707. The Borough Corporation agreed that £10 be given to anyone "who shall make discovery of the fires that have recently happened within the Borough". It was these fires which prompted the Corporation to establish the town's first fire brigade.

An order was made that "six large Iron Crooks shall be made for ye use of ye Corporation and twelve Leathron Buckets for use in case of Fire". In order to ensure a supply of water for the new fire service, it was ordered that "every householder within the Borough shall be obliged to keep two barrels of water at their doors or at the sides of their dwellings every day and night on ye penalty of 3s. 4d. for each householder that shall neglect".

The regulations made by the Corporation of Enniscorthy for fire-watching were specific:

> "It is ordered that there be always seven men on ye watch every night, that is, six men and one householder who is to command that night ye watch per turns three at a time and not to go from their watch till it be clear daylight."

The watch started at eight every night, and the watchers reported back regularly to "Mr Huson's little house". It was further decreed that "no householder shall be excused from the watch when it comes to his turn, if not an extraordinary occasion". If excused from the watch, the householder had to provide a suitable man in his place.

Enniscorthy then had a Corporation of its own with the full powers of a Corporate Borough, sending two members to the Irish Parliament. Its leading officials — the Portreeve, Clerk and Beadle (Sergeant of the Mace) — performed important judicial functions. In 1761, we are informed, the Corporation raised access on the Borough to have new stocks made. The prevailing atmosphere of the times is well illustrated by an entry in September, 1715:

> "Henry Coles was paid £3 by the Corporation for his expenses in hanging one Redmond, a Rapparee, who was executed at the request of the Portreeve and Burgesses."

After the abolition of the Corporation in 1840, there was a short period during which the town had no system of local government of its own, until the first Town Commissioners were established in 1851. The duties of the new Commissioners were limited to "the lighting, cleansing and watching of the town". The town rate then averaged sixpence in the pound.

The Urban Council was established in 1898. For two score years it tried, with varying degrees of success, to provide an adequate fire service. It was the custom of one time to sound the Cathedral bell at night to warn the townspeople that a serious fire had started. It was not until the early years of World War II that the present very efficient fire service was initiated, when a fire engine was purchased from Thurles Urban Council.

CX

ENNISCORTHY AND THE NATIONAL FLAG

Enniscorthy Town has a long and proud association with the history of the National Flag.

Readers may be familiar with the general history of the Tricolour. It was brought from Paris in 1848 by the deputation sent to convey the greetings of the Irish Confederation to the new French Republican Government after the overthrow of the monarchy in that year. Thomas Francis Meagher and William Smith O'Brien were members of this deputation. On their return they attended a reception given them by the citizens of Dublin, and Thomas Francis Meagher presented the chairman with a splendid flag which they had brought from Paris. Surmounted by an Irish pike, it was made of the richest French silk, which was most gorgeously trimmed and embroidered. The colours were orange, white and green. "From Paris, the gay and gallant city of the Tricolour and barricades, this flag has been proudly borne," said Meagher. The white in the centre signified a lasting truce between Orange and Green. "I trust," he said, "that beneath its folds the hands of the Irish Catholic and the Irish Protestant may be clasped in generous and heroic brotherhood". John Mitchell, referring to it, said: "I hope to see that flag one day waving as our national banner."

The date of the Dublin reception was April 15, 1848. This occasion has since been generally regarded as the first introduction of the Tricolour to Ireland.

Enniscorthy can claim that the Tricolour was displayed in the town six weeks before its presentation by Meagher to the Dublin meeting. On March 7, 1848, a demonstration was held in Enniscorthy to celebrate the success of the French Revolution in Paris. The *Freeman's Journal* of March 10 described the procession:

> "attended by an immense crowd at the head of which was carried a tricolour flag (the colours green, orange and white) which was frequently saluted by loud and rapturous acclamation."

The relevant quotation from the *Freeman's Journal* is as follows:

> "The men of Wexford have heard of the downfall of French tyranny with lively and heartfelt satisfaction. A spontaneous movement to celebrate this great triumph of freedom was made in this town on yesterday evening. Vinegar Hill had its brow crowned by a brilliant illumination which was visible from Mount Leinster to St George's Channel and was hailed by tens of thousands of "true men" as an omen of hope for fatherland. Our town was also lighted by bonfires in the Market Square and other quarters and enlivened by the temperance bands which played through the streets attended by an immense crowd at the head of whom was carried a tricolour flag (the colours green, orange and white) which was frequently saluted by loud and rapturous acclamation ..."

Attention was first drawn to this report in the *Freeman's Journal* in an article on the National Flag published in *An Cosantoir* (March, 1946). The author was Mr Patrick O'Connor, formerly Assistant Librarian in the National Library.

To supplement the information given in Mr O'Connor's article, it may be added that the local press gave a full report of the Enniscorthy demonstration. The *Wexford Guardian*, of date, Saturday, 11 March, 1848, under the heading:

Demonstration in Favour of the French Republic in Enniscorthy,
contained the following report:

> "An involuntary manifestation of popular feeling
> exhibited itself here on Tuesday night in
> commemoration of the glorious French Revolution, in
> the complete overthrow of the tyrant king, Louis
> Philippe, and the establishing of a Republican
> Government in its place. At an early hour in the
> evening, as if by magic, the town was illuminated
> with lighted tarbarrells, carried on men's shoulders,
> while several thousand persons of every sect and
> party marched in procession through the streets,
> followed by a handsome tricolour flag, composed of
> orange, white and green colours, and a band playing
> the most joyous and patriotic airs till a very late hour.
> Several shots were fired and the cheering of the crowd
> was excessive. The loud hurrahs for the glorious
> French, the French Revolution, the Repeal of the
> Union, and the union of all Irishmen of every sect and
> creed which rent the air were re-echoed at a great
> distance ..."

The demonstration was described in a report in John
Mitchel's newspaper, *The United Irishman,* of date March 11,
1848. Mention is again made of the carrying of "an Irish
tricolour — orange, green and white". The report is as
follows:

> "Enniscorthy — From seven o'clock until ten on
> Tuesday night, we had the amateur band parading the
> town, playing national airs followed by not less than
> three thousand persons, carrying an Irish tricolour —
> orange, green and white — and a half-dozen pitch-
> barrels. Six or eight of the latter were burned on
> Vinegar Hill; the night being very dark they had a
> splendid effect from that venerated eminence. There

were loud cheers for 'Repeal', 'The Young Republic',
'Down with British Rule.'"

— From a Correspondent.

Vinegar Hill is mentioned in all these reports. In July of
that year, Meagher and O'Brien were to pass by the hill,
when they came to Enniscorthy, preparatory to the Rising of
that year. They were on their way to the fateful scene at
Ballingarry, where "the Cause was lost again".

Meagher arrived on the night coach from Dublin
accompanied by John Blake Dillon. They ordered a car to
bring them to Maher's of Ballinkeele where Smith O'Brien
was staying since the previous day. John Maher of
Ballinkeele had become a member of the Irish Confederation
on March 23, 1848. While the car was getting ready, the two
men sat down before the Fire at Rudd's Hotel, and Maher
read for Dillon, an extract from *The Irish Fellow*, ending with
Lalor's noble appeal:

"Who will draw the first blood for Ireland? Who shall
win a wreath that shall be green for ever?"

"Passing out of the town," wrote Meagher, "the first
object which struck us was Vinegar Hill, with the old
windmill on the summit of it, sparkling in the morning light.
You can easily imagine the topic upon which our
conversation turned as we passed it by." In his *Personal
Narrative*, written in Richmond Prison in 1849, and addressed
to Charles Gavan Duffy, Meagher recalls his visit to
Enniscorthy. He says:

"Alas! It is a bitter thought with me, whilst I write
these lines — more bitter far, a thousand times, than
the worst privations of prison life — that, unlike those
gallant Wexfordmen of 1798, we have left behind us
no famous field within the length and breadth of the
old country, which men could point to with proud
sensation, and fair hands strew with garlands."

A flag of orange and green was carried at the great Amnesty Meeting held in the Abbey Square, Enniscorthy, on October 17, 1869, to urge the release of the Fenian prisoners. Reports in the local newspapers said that there were between forty and sixty thousand people present. After the meeting a section of the crowd, numbering ten thousand, marched four deep from the Abbey Square to Vinegar Hill.

> "The immense body of men, fine stalwart men, too, who stood on the plateau, reverently knelt, and with uncovered heads, offered up prayers for the dead who had suffered in the cause of Irish nationality."

When they arose from their knees they scattered themselves over the hill, and gathered fern and wildflower and pieces of stone as mementoes of this historic spot. Amongst the banners carried was one of orange and green, with the motto "Unity is Strength". The colour white is not mentioned. The Stars and Stripes were also carried on that occasion.

At that time and for many years afterwards the accepted national banner was the green flag with a yellow or gold harp. From the literature dealing with the 1798 Rising in Wexford it is quite clear that the green emblem or flag held undisputed sway. A very notable exception to this general rule must be mentioned here. It is contained in description of the Battle of Arklow, fought on June 9, 1798. The Wexfordmen carried a Tricolour banner with them into that battle. The information is contained in a letter, "Written on the Field of Battle", dated Arklow, June 13, 1798. The title of the letter says that it gives "some account of the Battle of Arklow, by H. G. of the Armagh Militia in a letter to a Friend in Dublin". The letter says:

> "On Saturday last we were informed that the Rebels in great force were pursuing us, the drums beat to arms and our forces assembled immediately. Our General formed a square of infantry at one end of the town, and left the Cavalry to defend the other. In a

little time, the Outposts were driven in, and shortly afterwards appeared, their Colours flying. They extended for more than five miles around us; a most awful sight! In order to intimidate us they fixed their hats on their pikes and rushed on.

"Their Artillery was planted on an eminence which commanded us — their armed men in front, and pike to charge in the rear. In this order of battle they came forward. We waited the first onset; in a few minutes the firing commenced in all quarters, which lasted from four o'clock in the afternoon till near nine at night. They endeavoured to break our square in every quarter, but like true soldiers we cleaved together and repelled them; they stormed our little line twice, but were beat back with slaughter; they drove their dismounted horses to the mouths of the Cannon in order to shelter themselves, but the grape shot made them fall on every side ... Flushed with victory at Gorey they thought that after they had taken Arklow nothing could stop them till they arrived at Dublin, and indeed, I believe, that this Battle for the present has decided the fate of this Kingdom.

"One of the Antrim Militia who fled from them after the Battle reports their Army to have been 20,000 strong. Among the slain was Fr Murphy from the County of Wexford. They lost about 1,000 killed and wounded, and numbers were hanged in the streets. Every Regiment vied with each other for victory; we took several stand of colours from them, made of green, white and yellow stuff ..."

It is reasonable to suggest that the carrying of the Tricolour by the Wexfordmen into Arklow reflects the emergence of United Irish influence in the Insurgent counsels. It may be added that two days earlier, June 7, the Insurgent leader, Edward Roche of Garrylough, addressed a proclamation to the people of Ireland; dated from Wexford, the proclamation says: "To promote a union of brotherhood and affection amongst our countrymen of all religious persuasions has been our principal object", words which summarise perfectly the sentiment symbolised by the Tricolour.

Enniscorthy was one of the few towns outside Dublin to join in the Insurrection of Easter Week, 1916. The Irish Volunteers in Enniscorthy rose on Thursday of that week (April 27), they had then headquarters at the Athenaeum Hall, Castle Street. On that morning a Tricolour flag of green, white and orange was raised over the building and suitable military honours were accorded to it. No other flag was raised over the building. The Tricolour had been extensively used as a patriotic emblem by the Separatist wing of the Volunteers during the years preceding the Rising.

ભ

APPENDIX

To the above notes may be added a further reference to the Tricolour brought from Paris by Meagher and Smith O'Brien. In 1852, Sir Francis B. Head published his Fortnight in Ireland, and there in p.102, 2nd Ed., he gives an account of his visit to the Police Headquarters in Dublin Castle:

> "In the police store, within its precincts, I found a number of trophies that had been obtained by the force. Among them was the Tricolour flag given by certain Paris ladies of easy political virtue to Mr Meagher, and captured in the summer of 1848."

Carried to battle by the Wexford Insurgents of 1798, and banned as an emblem of rebellion through the nineteenth century, the Green, White and Orange emerged as the National Flag in 1916.

Enniscorthy's association with the colours was fittingly commemorated on Easter Sunday, 1961, when the townspeople presented the Tricolour to St Aidan's Cathedral. The colours were blessed by Most Rev. Dr Staunton and accepted by his Lordship for the Cathedral, where they now hang above a plaque.

ᏸ

THE OLD THATCHED
CATHEDRAL OF ENNISCORTHY

On June 29, 1846, Mass was celebrated for the first time in St Aidan's Cathedral, Enniscorthy. The Cathedral was designed by Augustus Welby Pugin. For about 40 years previous to that date, there stood on the same site the old thatched Cathedral of Enniscorthy.

The bishop who was responsible for the erection of this thatched cathedral was Dr Patrick Ryan, Bishop of Ferns (1804-19). He had been parish priest of Clontarf Dublin; in the list of the bishops of Ferns he comes between Dr Caulfield and Dr Keating.

The thatched cathedral dated from 1808. In 1805, Fr William Synott, parish priest of Enniscorthy, died. Enniscorthy then became a mensal parish: the bishop is its parish priest. In 1806, Dr Ryan came to live in a house at Slaney Place, and in 1809 when work was completed on the thatched cathedral, Enniscorthy became the cathedral town of the Diocese of Ferns.

The thatched cathedral was a long, rectangular building. In *The Banks of the Boro*, Patrick Kennedy refers to "the big, diamond-shaped flags of the floor". In an advertisement in *The Wexford Herald*, dated June 19, 1806, I came across an interesting reference to the cathedral. It reads:

> "A house and garden to be let in Main Street, Enniscorthy, situated near the ground where the new chapel is going to be built."

The wording of this advertisement seems to suggest that the idea of building the cathedral was in the air from the time of Bishop Ryan's coming to live in Enniscorthy.

In 1852 when Richard Griffith's Primary Valuation Lists for County Wexford were published, Pugin's Cathedral had already been built, hence these lists are of no value when seeking information about the old thatched cathedral, but the latter building was still standing in 1838-9 when the preliminary surveys were being made for these Valuation Lists. From this unexpected source we can glean, therefore, a great deal of useful information, even on the exact dimensions of the old building. It filled, apparently, the same space approximately as that occupied by the nave of the Pugin Cathedral. It had a vestry room attached and a basement storey, and in the south end there was a gallery.

The Lancasterian School was situated a short distance away, but on the same site. It contained two rooms. This little building merits an article all to itself. At one time the Christian Brothers taught there. It later became the Enniscorthy Reading Rooms. There is nothing about the school in the archives of the Dept. of Education in Dublin (these archives used to be housed at Marlborough Street, but they are now in the Public Record Office in the Four Courts). This note says, under date 1850: "An apartment under the school room is used as a lumber room for the cathedral." In April, 1874, Fr Tom Burke, the famous Dominican, came to preach a sermon in the Cathedral; the report in *The Watchman* said that the clergy who took part in the ceremonies assembled first of all in the Reading Rooms before marching in procession to the cathedral.

The well-known traveller and topographer, John Bernard Trotter, writing in 1812 refers to the building as "an exceedingly large and handsome chapel," and he speaks of "the great Catholic population which attends it". The building of this thatched cathedral in 1808 was a historic event because it marked the re-establishment of full diocesan organisation after the Penal centuries.

In the cathedral there is a mural slab to the memory of Bishop Ryan. It tells that the date of his birth was 1768.

A mural slab of the same kind to Bishop Caulfield, the predecessor of Dr Ryan, is to be seen on the interior wall of the Franciscan Friary in Wexford. Any young student who is studying the careers of these two prelates should not fall into the error of making a facile judgement on the extent of their achievements without first considering the immensity of the difficulties these prelates had to face. There is a report in the *Wexford Evening Post* in January, 1828, of a meeting of the Catholic inhabitants of Enniscorthy in the cathedral to plead for Emancipation. Rev. George Whitty presided. At that period it was very common to hold meetings of that kind in parish churches.

In the Winter of 1837, a weakness was noticed in the roof of Bishop Ryan's Cathedral, and Dr James Keating, who had meanwhile succeeded to the See of Ferns, called a meeting of the Catholics of Enniscorthy to consider the matter. Dr Keating had been appointed co-adjutor Bishop two months before the death of Dr Ryan in 1819, and in March of that year he was consecrated Bishop of Ferns. At the meeting referred to Bishop Keating presided, and there was a long discussion on "the enlarging, improving and repairing" of the old thatched building which ultimately led to the plan for the building of the Pugin Cathedral. A year earlier, Dr Keating had laid the foundation stone of the chapel of St Peter's College. The designing of this chapel was the work of Augustus Welby Pugin. It is well to refer to the other churches in this diocese which were designed by Pugin — the churches in Gorey, Ramsgrange, Togoat and Barntown. Mention should also be made of Ballyhogue church. It is a source of pride to us that of all Pugin's Irish masterpieces, more than half of them are located in the Diocese of Ferns.

∞

In July, 1843, the foundation stone of St Aidan's Cathedral was laid, but it was not until June, 1846 that Mass was celebrated for the first time there. Pugin's Cathedral was erected on the same site as the old thatched building. The plan was to erect the new over the old, and while work progressed feverishly on the Pugin building the old cathedral remained in use. Finally the old cathedral was taken down and removed.

☙

One of the most treasured traditions of Enniscorthy is the picture of Bishop Keating moving through the fair, chatting with the farmers, asking one to bring a few cartloads of stones from the Abbey ground to the cathedral site, and urging another to bring a few loads of sand or lime from the riverside. These men regarded it as a privilege to do what the good bishop asked and it was through voluntary efforts of that kind that the total cost of the building was kept from soaring too high.

Before the erection of Dr Ryan's thatched cathedral, the needs of the Catholic people of Enniscorthy were served by two small chapels — one at Drumgoold, the other a small thatched structure at the end of Irish Street. The last occupant of the little house beside the site of the old chapel at Irish Street, the late Mr Michael Murphy, recorded for the Irish Folklore Commission the following tradition: On the day of the Battle of Vinegar Hill in 1798 a number of people were praying fervently in the chapel at Irish Street where they could hear the booming of artillery from the scene of the battle on the far side of the river. It was on this day precisely, that is June 21, 1798, that the chapel of Drumgoold was destroyed — the chapel was burned by a section of General Lake's troops.

In 1801 a new chapel was built at Chapel Lane, Drumgoold, to replace the burned chapel. By that time the old parish of Templeshannon had been united with that of Enniscorthy. Fr Francis Lacy was the last parish priest of the parish of Templeshannon. The late Rev. Joseph Ranson, Adm., Enniscorthy, loved to recall (he was a great admirer of

Drumgoold and its people) how the little Drumgoold
building, long after it had ceased to be used as a church,
came to be utilised during the years of the Famine as a centre
for the teaching of Catechism on Sundays to Catholic
children.

My friend, Mr Matty O'Neill, who is a native of the Irish
Street, reminded me last week of the old tradition that the
double doorway in Mr Michael Redmond's house in Irish
Street is a relic of an old right-of-way from the cathedral site
to the chapel at the Irish Street. The genial sacristan of the
cathedral, Mr Edward (Ned) Earle, who also knows old
Enniscorthy well, has been good enough to point out to me
that this pathway served a second purpose in later times —
that is, when Bishop Michael Warren lived in Slaney Lodge,
this path-way was for him a short-cut when he was going to
the cathedral daily to celebrate Mass.

The story of these small chapels at Irish Street and at
Drumgoold, and of Bishop Ryan's old thatched cathedral, is
a chapter of Enniscorthy history which, like the story of the
Franciscan Friary, deserves to be faithfully remembered.

ଔ

THE SCHOOL BESIDE THE CHAPEL

A NEGLECTED CHAPTER OF IRISH EDUCATIONAL HISTORY

In writings on the subject of primary education in modern Ireland a certain set sequence in its development has come to be accepted. It is the purpose of this short article to suggest that some revision is necessary in the presentation of the main facts in this field of study. If we commence with the Penal Laws in the eighteenth century, we learn first of all of the decline of the native Schools, followed by the emergence of the famous Hedge-schools, leading in the 1830s to the advent of the National Schools under the direct control of the National Board of Education. Reference is seldom made to the important part played by the Chapel Schools. This is a serious omission as can be seen from a study of schools in the Diocese of Ferns and we can assume that the same thing holds true for other parts of Catholic Ireland.

In the matter of time, the School beside the Chapel falls between the Hedge-schools and the National Schools, for the teachers who taught in these schools were often men who had spent years as hedge-schoolmasters and ultimately these Chapel Schools in many parishes became merged in the National School system. In 1837 a traveller who was by no means friendly to the claims of Catholic education wrote a letter from Enniscorthy in which he stated:

> "Now if I see a Romish chapel, I find some new spruce building within the very precincts of its boundary, a school, and what is the system of instruction adopted there? The Bible is excluded; a

mutilated extract, unfaithful even in its mutilation, is substituted nominally ... and in a multitude of instances, the person appointed to the office of Master is a furious zealot in popery and sedition."[1]

Walks Through Ireland by John Bernard Trotter is a valuable source-book on many aspects of our local history, including education. Travelling on the road from Bunclody to New Ross in 1812, Trotter remarked: "We observed schools at all the chapels as we walked along and education attended to very generally."[2] The Chapel Schools are frequently referred to in the works of Patrick Kennedy. In his chapter on The School of Rathnure in *The Bank of the Boro*,[3] Kennedy gives us a comparison between the Chapel Schools and the Hedge-schools. The Rathnure school was accommodated "in a small house in the corner of the Chapel yard at Rathnure". Kennedy goes on to inform his readers:

> "The Rathnure School was in the extent of its accommodations, one step higher than the unsophisticated Hedge-school in which the seats consisted of stones covered with dry scraws or sods. It had some wooden seats though it had not reached the dignity of a table. There was a single chair for the Master's use and his first occupation on taking possession of it in the morning after hearing the tasks was to make or mend the pens of all who had attained to the dignity of the writing class."

Arithmetic, book-keeping and mensuration were some of the subjects learned by the advanced pupils who varied from thirteen to twenty years of age.

I have found the most useful source of information on the Chapel Schools to be the National Education Papers[4] in the Public Record Office in Dublin. Relying on this latter source alone, there was a school beside the chapel in each of the following centres: Askamore, Murrintown, Kingsland, Kiltealy, Cullenstown, the Female School at Adamstown and the Male Schools at Kilmuckridge, New Ross, Ballygarret and Bunclody.

With regard to the Adamstown Female School the local Inspector reported to the National Board on 22 November 1844, that "a dinner was given in the school in honour of Fr Mathew on 10th inst". The Manager was informed by the Board that this was an infringement of Rule 1143 of the Board. The Manager promised not to violate this rule in future. Regarding Bunclody Male School there is a note at the top of the folio that "this school is built on Chapel ground. The school first received a grant from the board in August 1842".

In the case of Clologue school, a note says: "This school is attached to the Chapel. There is a connection between it and the Chapel but it will be closed." It was a one-roomed school, 16 feet square. The teacher's name was John Byrne. The Board wrote to Rev. Thomas Pierce stating that the connection between the school and the chapel must be closed up, "otherwise the Board's grant cannot be continued". The school first received aid from the Board in November 1840. Rev. Daniel Kavanagh wrote to the Board intimating that the connection between the school and the chapel would be closed up.

There is an interesting point in a letter sent by the Board to the Superioress of Gorey Convent School on 31 October 1854:

> "The practice of the children blessing themselves whenever the clock strikes must be discontinued; this practice as well as the repetition of the Angelus and all other religious exercises must be confined to the time notified on the Time Table as being set apart for religious instruction."

On 30 April 1852 the Inspector reported on the Mercy Convent School in Wexford, stating that the lower room of the school was used on the first Sunday of each month as a Circulating Library; also that when the clock strikes the teachers and scholars repeat the "Hail Mary" and cross themselves. The Board informed the Manager that "however laudable the purpose a Circulating Library serves, it is a violation of the rules of the Board, and therefore the Commissioners request that the practice be discontinued. The practice as to prayer is not considered a violation of the rules as it is repeated mentally". In the following year, however, the Board requested the Inspector to inform the Manager that the Commissioners object to prayers being said at several times during ordinary school hours. "Prayers should be said only at the time set apart for religious instruction on the Time Table."

Of New Ross Male School we are told that "this school had been established in 1819 and was connected with the chapel". In 1838 a complaint was made to the Board that their rules had been violated when a political meeting was held in the school. The Board subsequently received a reply, regarding this complaint, admitting that a meeting was held but stating that it was not considered political as it was held only for the purpose of returning thanks to Mr O'Connell for putting down combinations of works.[5]

Numerous references to the Great Famine turn up in these records. On one occasion in 1847, when the Inspector visited Ballindaggin School, he found that the Famine Relief Committee of the district had held a meeting in the school on that day and consequently the children were not asked to attend. The Inspector's report on Clologue School on 30 September 1847, stated: "This school is closed since the end of August, fever being prevalent in the neighbourhood." The cholera is specifically mentioned in an Inspector's report on Kilmuckridge Male School dated 1 March 1850. He says that the school had been closed for the previous fortnight by the Manager "in consequence of cholera prevailing in the village".

Kilmuckridge Male School was built on chapel ground. The dimensions of the schoolroom were 26½ feet by 13 feet. The teacher's name was Edward O'Connor. Aid received from the National Board commenced in August 1848 and was limited to the supply of books to 100 boys. At the very same time, the Board also provided books to 100 pupils of Kilmuckridge Female School in which Catherine O'Connor was the teacher. Rev. J. Sinnot is named as the Manager. In March 1850 the Inspector reported that this school was also closed "because the teacher is at present labouring under the prevailing cholera". Due to illness the teacher discontinued her teaching career in July 1852. Later Bridget O'Connor was appointed in her place.

There was an Evening School attached to Bunclody Male School. The Inspector reported in 1850 that the Evening School closed on 26 March "owing to the prevalence of cholera". Several times the name of the famous Fr James Parle is mentioned in these educational records. He became Manager of the Bunclody school in October 1849 when Fr James Walsh, P.P., was transferred to New Ross. On 14 August 1851 we are informed that Fr Parle is leaving the parish and is resigning the management of the school to Rev. F. Wafter, P.P. It is noted on top of the folio that this school is built on chapel ground and first received aid from the Board in August 1842.[6]

The references to the Great Famine found in these Education Papers help to bring out two important points about the Famine in County Wexford; first, that the evil effects of the Famine did not end in 1847 but lasted for several years afterwards, and secondly, that the effects of the Famine were felt more sorely in North Wexford, a fact which is borne out by the statistical and other evidence. The reader will notice that the centres mentioned — Clologue, Bunclody, Ballindaggin and Killmuckridge — are all in North Wexford.

Other schoolhouses mentioned as being built on chapel ground include Kingsland and Glenbrien. A note on Glenbryan School (it is so spelt) says that it was built on chapel ground but separated from the chapel by a wall. The schoolhouse at Cullenstown was actually attached to the chapel. A note on Bree Male School says that it was held in an old church, converted for the purpose. The teacher's name was James Kerevan, aged forty-five.

Special attention needs to be paid to the large schoolhouse built by Dr Keating in the grounds of the Pugin Cathedral at Enniscorthy. This was a slated building in which the boys of the parish were educated. An apartment under the schoolroom was used as a lumber-room for the Cathedral. The average attendance in April 1850 was 140. When the Irish Christian Brothers first come to Enniscorthy in 1857 they commenced their work at the Cathedral School.

The girls of the parish attended the Presentation Convent School. In 1826 Dr Keating, Bishop of Ferns, brought the Presentation Sisters to Enniscorthy. He placed his residence in Weafer Street at their disposal and in this building they lived and laboured until July 1840 when they removed to a new site, where the present Convent stands.

Thomas Lacy's *Sights and Scenes of Our Fatherland*, published in 1863, is a book which sums up admirably educational conditions in Enniscorthy at that time:

> "There is a large school, in connection with the National Board of Education, immediately adjoining the Cathedral grounds ... The Convent of the nuns of the Presentation Order, with their fine chapel and nice school, is favourably situated at a short distance West of the Cathedral and commands an excellent view of the river and the handsome seats that ornament its banks."[7]

Under date August 1843 there is a useful account of the Presentation Convent School in the Valuation Papers in Dublin. It states:

> "The school-room and chapel are one house, the upper storey is used as a chapel and the under as a schoolroom."[8]

The National Education Papers in PRO, Dublin, in addition to their value as a very good source for educational history, provide us incidentally with useful information on other aspects of our local history. For example, a note on Sion National School in 1853 says that Devereux's Catechism was then used in that school.

Of wider interest is the story of the teacher at Ballymurn. This school had a unique feature due to the fact that the Manager appointed to the schoolhouse was a layman — Mr John Maher of Ballinkeele. The Board undertook to pay the teacher's salary as from 1 June 1847. The teacher's name was Stenson McIver. In August 1848, the Board received a letter from T. B. Redington, Esq., Dublin Castle, enclosing a copy of a Public Report relative to Mr McIver. The Board wrote to the Manager stating that the Commissioners had before them the Inspector's report concerning the charge preferred against Mr McIver in being concerned in the purchase of swords which it is supposed were intended to be used for an improper purpose. The Commissioners approve of the Inspector's action in dismissing him from charge of the school. They felt it their duty to dismiss him from the Board's service as from 1 August 1841. Mr Maher made a strong plea for the teacher but his efforts were in vain.

The teacher's name in Oulart was James O'Brien. A note in the National Education Papers under date 1850 says that there were three hedge-schools in operation in the neighbourhood. One was in Ballinamona, the second at Kilcotty, the third at Oulartwick.

There is no need to give any further facts to bring out the point which I sought at the outset to establish — the importance of the Chapel Schools in the educational history of the Diocese of Ferns in the first half of the nineteenth century. I have relied mainly on one source of information, that is the National Education Papers. I make no claim to have given an exhaustive list of the Chapel Schools in the Diocese and undoubtedly other useful sources can be utilised to supplement the list. The two standard sources on educational history in the first half of the nineteenth century are the Irish Education Inquiry of 1826 (Second Report) and the Report of the Commissioners on Public Instruction 1835.

CB

---

[11] *Letters from Ireland* dated 1837; written by Charlotte Elizabeth. Published by R. B. Seeling and W. Burnside. Sold by L. And G. Seeling, Feet Street, London. The book contains 436 pages. The letter from Enniscorthy is on page 46.

[2] *Walks Through Ireland* (1812-19) by John Bernard Trotter.

[3] See page 254 of the 1867 edition of *The Banks of the Boro*.

[4]*The National Education Papers* in the Public Record Office in Dublin. For the period 1835-55, County Wexford is covered by one large volume of bound registers and extracts, which is numbered 2C — 57 — 64. When I first studied these records they were housed in the offices of An Roinn Oideachais in Marlborough Street, but they have since been transferred to the Public Record Office at the Four Courts.

[5]It is a leading feature of Industrial History that Daniel O'Connell was a strong opponent, during his years in the House of Commons, of Trade Unions, then usually called "combinations of workers".

[6]Fr James Parle figures prominently in the history of County Wexford in the middle of the last century. While a curate in Enniscorthy he was a staunch supporter of 'Young Ireland'. He is honoured by the fact that his name is mentioned in Michael Doheny's *The Felon's Track*. His name is associated with the coming of the Faithful Companions of Jesus to Bunclody and the early history of St Mary's Convent. He went to Australia to collect funds for the extension of convent. He spent several years in Australia and in 1870 he received a severe fall from his horse and died at Melbourne from his injuries on 29 March of the year.

He built St Patrick's Church, Port Fairy, Victoria. There is a fine memorial erected over his grave at Tower Hill, Port Fairy. The inscription on the memorial says that he died in his 58th year. I find a note in my notebook, copied from *The Wexford Guardian*, which states that on 1 July 1848, Fr Parle, then of Enniscorthy, attended a meeting of County Wexford Repeal Club accompanied by Mr Anthony O'Hara, who was then on the staff of St Peter's College, Wexford. Mr O'Hara conducted his own Classical and Commercial school in Guttle Street, Enniscorthy for many years. He is one of those people who subscribed to Dr Keating's fund for the erection of St Aidan's Cathedral. With regard to Fr Parle's career, it is a matter of regret that no comprehensive article has yet been written on him. I am indebted to two sources for the little information given above — (1) *Bun Clóidí, A History of the District* by an tAthair Séamas S. De Vál, *Bun Clóidí* 1966, *arna chló go príobháideach*, and (2) Mr Fintan Murphy of the Castle Museum who learned a good deal about Fr Parle from a distinguished Australian visitor, Rev. Brother E. B. Doyle. There is a portrait of Fr Parle in the FCJ Convent in Bunclody. The portrait is hanging in a place of honour. Through the kindness of the Rev. Mother Superior, permission was given to Mr Colum Breen to paint a copy of the portrait. The copy made by Mr Breen now hangs in the County Museum.

[7] *Sights and Scenes of Our Fatherland* by Thomas Lacy, Wexford, Published 1863. 720 pages. Two entire chapters are devoted to County Wexford.

[8] This information is gleaned from the Field Books of *Griffith's Primary Valuation of Ireland*, preserved in Ely Place, Dublin.

ରଷ

THE CHRISTIAN BROTHERS IN
ENNISCORTHY, 1857-1957

The school beside the chapel was a familiar scene in Ireland in the years between the Union and the Famine. Throughout the eighteenth century the hedge schools had done excellent work for education; but now the Penal enactments against Catholic teaching had been repealed; the hedge schoolmasters could come into the open, and the Church was free to undertake the buildings of schools, a tremendous task at a time when the erection of churches was already straining the slender resources of every Catholic parish. It was against the background that the small schoolhouse arose in the corner of the chapel grounds, oftentimes a single-roomed thatched building, built and maintained by the generous contributions of an impoverished people, without any State assistance.

The Irish people distrusted the State-endowed schools; their attitude is well summed up in the letter written by the Bishop of Ferns, Most Rev. Dr Ryan. "The parents are more inclined," he wrote, "to have their children uneducated that run the risk of having them proselytised ... The Board of Education will make little progress till they give up the idea of making proselytes instead of scholars." It was imperative that an independent school system should be established to protect the Faith of the children. For this reason chapel schools were established, and it was for precisely the same reasons that Edmund Ignatius Rice gave up his wealth to devote himself to education of the Catholic youth of Ireland, opening his first school at Mount Sion, Waterford, in 1804.

Enniscorthy had its own chapel school. It stood in the grounds of the old thatched cathedral which had been erected in 1808. The principal classroom in the schoolhouse was 54 feet long and 24 feet wide. The building cost £900 to erect, and in 1826 there was an attendance of 156 boys there. By the year 1850, the present cathedral had been built on the site of the old. Up to 1826 there was also a girls classroom in the school, accommodating over a hundred pupils.

The cathedral schoolhouse was built by Most Rev. Dr Keating, who was consecrated Bishop of Ferns in 1819. It was he who undertook the erection of St Aidan's Cathedral, and also laid the foundations of the modern educational system in Enniscorthy parish. He was an enthusiastic supporter of Daniel O'Connell, and a vigorous opponent of the National School system as introduced under Whately and Carlisle. In 1826 he brought the Presentation Sisters of Enniscorthy, the first of the teaching Orders to come: he gave them his own house in Weafer Street as a residence, which he had acquired from the Lett family shortly before. The girls' school at the cathedral was closed and their education entrusted to the nuns. In 1840, the Presentation school was transferred to the present site. An inspector who visited the school in 1850 reported:

> "The schoolroom and chapel are one house, the upper storey is used as a chapel, and the under as a schoolroom ... The books used in the school are those of the Christian Brothers."

Dr Keating died in 1849 and in his will he left £1,000 to be used to bring the Irish Christian Brothers to Enniscorthy. He had already introduced them to the towns of Wexford and New Ross.

Most Rev. Dr Furlong became Bishop of Ferns early in 1857 and he lost no time in extending an invitation to the Brothers to establish a community here. And so it was that Brother Philip Slattery, accompanied by one assistant, Brother Anthony Cogan, arrived in Enniscorthy on

September 1, 1857. Their first task was to take charge of the cathedral schoolhouse, "the school beside the chapel".

A native of Bruff, Co. Limerick, Brother Slattery had been recalled from the English Mission in order to establish the new community. He had done splendid work for the poor of Dublin during the Great Famine. He died at New Ross 40 years later at the age of 78.

Enniscorthy at that period was a town of small industries and house crafts, depending upon the agricultural community for its prosperity. Six years earlier Town Commissioners had been established and the streets lit by gas for the first time. Six further years had to elapse before the Dublin railway was extended to the town, which was still suffering from the effects of the Famine. Its population had dwindled from 7,016 in 1841 to 5,396 in 1861.

The first residence occupied by the Brothers was a humble dwelling in the backyard of Mr O'Dempsey's house at 10 Rafter Street. After two years they moved to a house in Upper Weafer Street. A "house which had a few trees and a small lawn in front". In 1858, Dr Furlong brought the Sisters of Mercy to Enniscorthy where they taught at a temporary building at the Shannon. In the following year the bishop erected at The Shannon a new school containing two classrooms for the education of the boys of that district, and two additional Brothers came to take charge. For some time there were two Christian Brothers' schools in Enniscorthy, one at the cathedral under Brother Slattery and the other at The Shannon. According to the 1861 census the Brothers had 151 pupils in their Shannon schools, and 221 at the cathedral.

In 1863 there were 216 girls on the rolls of the Mercy School. An inspector's report said:

"Previous to 1859, the educational needs of this part of the town were so neglected that the Catholic bishop decided on establishing schools for boys and girls. Separate schoolrooms were accordingly built on opposite sides of the street, the boys' school being

placed under the care of the Christian Brothers, that of
the girls under the Sisters of Mercy."

A contemporary topographer, writing in 1863, says:

"A branch of the devoted Sisters of Mercy at Wexford
has recently been established here and consists at
present of three of the nuns, who reside in a very neat
cottage in the northern suburbs. Their school is
situated at the Shannon on the opposite side of the
river, closely adjoining the Christian Brothers' School,
a new and commodious house."

In 1860 Brother John Norris succeeded Brother Slattery as
Superior. In the same year the Brothers transferred their
residence from Weafer Street to a house at Templeshannon
— "a decaying house next to the graveyard," Brother Norris
describes it, "called the Abbey". In a very interesting set of
family accounts books, dating back for more than a century,
preserved by Mr Michael J. Jordan, Market Square, several
entries refer to — "Brother Norris, The Monastery". An entry
dated November 2, 1863, reads — "Mr Norris, Abbey House,
1lb. tea, 3s. 8d".

The Brothers resided in this house at Templeshannon for
several years. In 1866 Dr Furlong approved of a proposal
made by Brother Norris to purchase a plot of ground on
Island Road for the building of a combined residence and
schools for the Brothers. The reason given by Brother Norris
for the selection of that particular site was the fact that it was
near the Bridge, and hence the children from The Shannon
would not have to walk too far to school. The Brothers'
school at The Shannon was to be handed over to the Sisters
of Mercy. Three or four cabins on the Island Road site were
demolished, and Mr Wilkinson contracted to erect the new
building for £1,000. Work was commenced in 1866 and the
Brothers went into residence early in 1867. For almost thirty
years the upper portion of the new building was used as a
residence, the lower part as classrooms.

Brother Norris during his term in Enniscorthy endeared himself to all sections of the people. Of all the early Brothers his was the name best loved and longest remembered. A man of high administrative ability and pleasing disposition, he spent twelve years as Superior and laboured tirelessly to provide sound education for the boys of the district. In later years he was loud in his praise of the Enniscorthy people and their generosity towards the Brothers. In 1872 he was transferred to Rathkeale and after a career of fruitful toil he died in the monastery at Wexford in 1913, aged eighty-nine years. During the early part of his period in Enniscorthy one of the Brothers in his community was Brother Philip Holland, who in later years became famous in the United States of America as the inventor of the submarine.

In the annals of the Enniscorthy monastery the same entry which chronicles the departure of Brother Norris records the coming of the Loreto Nuns to Enniscorthy in October, 1872. They resided in the house in Weafer Street that had been occupied in the 1830s by the Presentation Order and used in the intervening years as a school by John O'Meagher. They were the last of the great teaching Orders to arrive in the town, thus completing the magnificent work done by Dr Furlong, one of the greatest bishops of Ferns, for the parish of Enniscorthy which included the establishment of the House of Missions, the building of the Shannon Chapel, and the introduction of three teaching Orders to the town.

It is a singular distinction of the Loreto Convent that it is intimately associated with two glorious names in the religious history of Ireland — Edel Quinn, the heroic Legion of Mary envoy to Africa who was a pupil there for some time, and Mother Mary Gonzaga Barry, who was its first Superioress and who did wonderful pioneering work in the establishment of the Loreto Order on the continent of Australia.

Mother Mary Gonzaga's biographer informs us that as early as 1872 and 1873 the Missionaries of the Blessed Sacrament used to come to celebrate Mass in the convent each morning. One of these priests was Fr Michael Kelly,

later to become Archbishop of Sydney. Mother Mary
Gonzaga toiled zealously until she had passed her fourscore
years in far-off Australia, and had the consolation in her last
illness of a visit from Dr Kelly. "That was a friendship that
had its roots in Enniscorthy by the winding Slaney," says her
biographer, "and that now proved itself by this special visit
from Sydney when Dr Kelly came to offer the Holy Sacrifice
of the Mass in her room". His Grace called to the Christian
Brothers' Schools on several occasions when he came to
Enniscorthy to visit the House of Missions. On September 11,
1901, he addressed the boys on Temperance and imparted
the Apostolic Benediction. Both he and Fr James A. Cullen,
SJ, were past pupils of the New Ross Brothers. In April, 1932,
the late Dr Rd. J. Downey Archbishop of Liverpool, visited
the schools at the Island Road where he had been a pupil for
a short time when he lived in Enniscorthy. Another
distinguished prelate received at the schools was Dr Daniel
Mannix, Archbishop of Melbourne, the great Irish patriot,
during his Irish tour of 1925, when Brother Crofts was
Superior.

It would be impossible in the course of a short article to
mention the large numbers of distinguished pupils who have
passed through the schools or to treat individually of the
magnificent work accomplished by succeeding Superiors in
improving the educational facilities for the boys of
Enniscorthy.

Brother Norris was succeeded in turn by Brother Colman
Flood, Brother Vincent Timmons and Brother Anthony
O'Sullivan. Brother Flood extended the school and by
acquiring two small houses "purchased with the funds
arising from school pence". Further improvements were
carried out on the Island Road building by Brother John
Redmond, who became Superior in 1877. A splendid teacher.
Brother Redmond's name was fondly remembered by
Enniscorthy men of the last generation. His family had
strong local associations, for three of his uncles had been
killed at the Battle of Vinegar Hill.

In 1880 Brother John Mark O'Byrne was appointed Superior. During those years Brother Justin Ryan was a member of the Enniscorthy community. Later he had a very distinguished career as Superior of several important houses in Ireland. Patrick Donovan records that Brother Ryan was deeply attached to the people of Enniscorthy and "for well nigh fifty years every St Patrick's Day an ex-pupil of his from that town used to send him a spray of shamrock plucked from historic Vinegar Hill".

Brother Dominic Kelly was Superior from 1888-97. The attendance at the schools had been increasing and the classrooms at Island Road were overcrowded. To relieve this problem, the Brothers made a great sacrifice by leaving their residence there and taking up their abode temporarily in two new houses at Munster Hill, the property of Mr F. Godfrey. Shortly afterwards Brother Kelly acquired the present monastery side from the then Earl of Portsmouth. When the agent, Mr George Roberts, was handing over this site in 1894 it is recorded in the annals for that year that he passed this remark to Brother Kelly: "The day is not long distant when the Government will be glad to hand over the Model School to the Christian Brothers." This prophecy was fulfilled half a century later. The contractor, Mr W. Fortune, commenced work on the erection of the new monastery at Mill Park Road in June, 1894, and completed the task in July of the following year.*

Then for the first time after 40 years in Enniscorthy the Brothers had, due to the efforts of Brother Kelly, secured a proper residence where they could carry out the rule of their Congregation in surroundings that provided at least a modicum of comfort. It we wish to get a clear picture of the discomforts suffered by the Brothers in their early years, we could not do better than quote the plain unadorned language of Brother Norris himself written years afterwards:

---

* Due to a decline in vocations, the Brothers left this monastery in the 1980s. It lay vacant for several years; it now houses The 1798 Museum.

"The members of the community lived a while in the
upper floor of a mealstore, at another time in a narrow
wretched house in New Street, at another time in a
decaying house near the graveyard, filled with rats,
and called the Abbey."

These wanderings came to an end when the new
monastery was completed in 1895.

Meanwhile the upper portion of the Island Road building
was refitted for classwork. Brother Dominic Kelly left
Enniscorthy in 1897 and in later years did notable work in
charge of the Artane Band. He died in 1920.

The improvements carried out by Brother Kelly opened
the way for excellent scholastic successes in the years that
followed under splendid teachers like Brother Leahy, Brother
Hoctor and Brother Curtin. Numerous exhibitions were won
in the intermediate examinations. It may be added here that
when the intermediate system was first introduced, St
Aidan's Academy carried out most of the secondary
education of the town. When Brother J. C. Hogan became
Superior in 1904, the high standard of education of the school
was further enhanced. He was again Superior from 1910-16
and remained as a teaching member of the community until
1920. A man of tall stature and commanding presence, his
name became a household word in Enniscorthy district, and
his achievements have become part of the town's history in
the first two decades of the century. A distinguished member
of Brother Hogan's community at that time was Brother M. S.
Kelly.

Brother Mulhall was Superior from 1907-10; when
Superior in Doneraile, he was an intimate friend of the late
Canon P. A. Sheehan.

Brother Crofts, Superior from 1923-28, was in charge of
the schools when they first became attached to the
Department of Education, in August, 1925. For over a
century prior to this, under the British régime, the Brothers
had held their primary schools aloof from the State system, a

position which changed only with the advent of a native Government.

Mention should also be made of three members of Brother Cofts' community — Brother M. P. Lynch and Brother M. L. O'Shea, whose work for Gaelic pastimes in the town is well remembered, and Brother M. S. Flately, who became a distinguished Irish scholar and who won the coveted Mansion House scholarship awarded by the National University for eminence in Celtic studies.

Other recent Superiors were Brother O'Mahoney (1916-23), Brother Lucey (1928-31), Brother Wilson (1931-4).

In 1934, Brother John McGovern's term commenced. By that time the Island Road buildings had deteriorated seriously. The schools had become dilapidated and unhealthy; their condition was aggravated by overcrowding, for the numbers attending the schools had more than doubled in 20 years. The community were working under intolerable conditions, and Brother McGovern took the initial steps towards the provision of a new primary school and the transfer of the Model School site to the Brothers. In all his efforts he had the enthusiastic co-operation of V. Rev. John Dean Codd, PP, VG, Ferns, who was then Administrator of the cathedral parish. All building operations were halted as a result of the outbreak of World War II and further progress could not be made until hostilities ended.

Brother McGovern's term ended in 1940 and he was succeeded by Brother J. G. Ennis. When the war ended, Brother Ennis lost no time in urging Enniscorthy's claim to a new school. A man of tireless energy, he brought the matter to a successful conclusion after long and protracted negotiations. The Government handed over the Model School to the Christian Brothers and plans were approved for the building of a new primary school to accommodate 500 pupils.

Brother Ennis remained a member of the community when Brother J. C. O'Flynn commenced his term as Superior in 1946. On the shoulders of the new Superior fell the heavy burden of the erection of the new school which cost £40,000.

On May 19, 1948, the late Rev. P. Quaid (later pastor of Piercestown) cut the first sod and on September 8 of the same year Most Rev. Dr Staunton, Bishop of Ferns, laid the foundation stone of the new schools. The building was blessed and officially opened by his lordship the bishop on Easter Sunday, 1950. This historic occasion was a great landmark in the annals of Catholic education in the town. It was the reward for long years of hard work on the part of successive Superiors. To less farsighted men the difficulties would have appeared insurmountable; the completion of the new school was a magnificent triumph, a fitting culmination to years of patient toil and Herculean effort, especially on the part of the two Superiors primarily responsible for the provision of the school — Brother Ennis and Brother O'Flynn.

ଓଷ

THE POPULATION OF COUNTY WEXFORD IN THE 17th CENTURY

The population of County Wexford reached its peak in the years immediately preceding the Great Famine, 1845-8. The figure for the county in 1841 was 202,033; at that date the population of Ireland was over eight millions.[1] In 1788, Bushe had made an estimate based on the returns of the Hearthmoney Collectors[2] and gave the number of people in County Wexford at that date as 132,912. There is evidence from several sources that this estimate may have been slightly below the truth,[3] and the available testimony points to the conclusion that in the year of the Rising the population of the county was not less than 150,000. In 1821 the figure was 170,806[4] which by 1841, as already stated, had exceeded 200,000. Then came the Great Famine, with all its tragic consequences. The outstanding importance of this great landmark in our county's story will be realised from the fact that within 15 years the county was bled of no fewer than 60,000 of its inhabitants.[5] The decline in population, though on a much more gradual scale, continued in the subsequent decades and at every decennial enumeration since 1851 a fall in the number of inhabitants has been recorded. In 1946 the figure had dropped to 91,855. An examination of the statistics reveals that the decrease since 1851 is attributable almost entirely to emigration, with which the study of population statistics in this country is always closely related.[6]

These facts relating to the last century and a half have been set down here by way of introduction, in order to help towards a clearer appreciation of the main trends in earlier centuries. Prior to 1788, when Bushe made his estimate, it is seldom that exact statistics are available; material is often so incomplete as to make it difficult to reach accurate conclusions; the student has to rely on references found here and there in the contemporary sources, in order to trace the main tendencies that were at work. The matter in this article had been compiled by the writer as part of a regional study in economic history from 1600 to the present day; but in these pages our purpose is limited to forming an estimate of the density and distribution of the population of County Wexford in the seventeenth century, as far as the materials will permit. Brief reference will be made to important factors bearing on the subject, such as emigration, incidence of famine and fever, the growth of towns, the ebb and flow of agricultural prosperity. Because of its well-defined boundaries, County Wexford is ideally suited for studies of this kind, and the examination of demographic changes becomes much more interesting as the unit of investigation becomes smaller.

∝

We have the opinion of several excellent authorities that the population of Ireland during medieval times was much less than that of the past two centuries. "There is no evidence of a continuous increase in the population of rural Ireland in medieval times," says Professor Eoin MacNeill. "In fact, epidemics and probably a high rate of infant mortality must have tended to keep the number at a level century after century."[7] Professor MacNeill goes on to estimate the average number of inhabitants in each Tuath at about 25,000, which would indicate a total population of less than two millions. Several other historians could be quoted in support of the same opinion.[8]

These epidemics mentioned by Professor MacNeill were not without their effects on Wexford, a fact which is apparent from numerous entries in the records of the county. Confining our attention to the sixteenth century, we have, for instance, in *Hore's History of Ross*, under date 1520, this informative note under the heading — "Pestilence in Ross" (Surrey writing to Woolsey):

"There is marvellous death in all this country, which is so sore that all the people be fled out of their houses into the fields and woods where they likewise die wonderfully, so that the bodies lie dead, like swine unburied."[9]

Again in 1552, Lord Deputy Crofte, writing to the Privy Council from Ross on April 16 of that year, says:

"The clamours of the poor artificers, who live in towns, and are reduced to extreme hunger by means of the great scarcity, soundeth continually in mine ears."[10]

In 1575 County Wexford is specifically mentioned amongst the parts of South Leinster which suffered from a great pestilence.[11]

It is clear from contemporary accounts that Wexford did not escape the ravages and destruction of Elizabeth's reign (1558-1603). As if to strike the keynote of that era, a special Commission was issued "to execute martial law in the territories of Fasaghbentry and the Moroes Country upon all persons ... found to be felons, rebels, enemies, or notorious malefactors, and to punish them by death or otherwise ..."[12]

In 1579 a petition was sent from the inhabitants of the Southern Baronies, and Hore comments on the idea it gives of the scanty population and poverty of the south of the county at this period.[13]

The situation in North Wexford was much worse. Here the ruthless efforts of the Tudor forces to bring the Gaelic families to submission resulted in a state of perpetual warfare for several decades. The Kavanaghs stubbornly resisted the attempts of Elizabeth to force them to accept a religious and political system that was abhorrent to them. These disturbances could not fail to have widespread repercussions on economic conditions in all that rich territory; during the Nine Years' War the Kavanaghs allied themselves with the Northern Chieftains. *The Irish Annals*, under date 1580, give us a glimpse of the disturbed conditions in Southern Leinster in the Elizabethan age:

> "The entire extent of country from the Slaney to the Shannon, and from the Boyne to the Meeting of the Three Waters became one scene of strife and dissension."[14]

The families specifically mentioned as participating in this struggle on the Catholic side include "Kavanaghs and Kinsellas, O'Byrnes and O'Tooles". The Elizabethan conquerors were determined to smash the power of these Gaelic families. "There is no way to daunt these people but by the edge of the sword," wrote Sir Henry Wallop to Walsingham in 1581. The effects of this policy may be judged from a letter written by the same gentleman five years later. "The want of provisions is greatly felt," he says. "The soldiers have had no corn these four days."[15] In the following year (1587), again referring to Enniscorthy, he says: "The place being altogether waste, with the country round about it, even to the gates of Wexford." How deplorable conditions were in the neighbourhood of Enniscorthy in that year can be realised from the fact that provisions were so difficult to procure that the garrison had to have food sent from Dublin.[16] The vessel came from Dublin to Wexford, and the provisions were despatched up the Slaney to Enniscorthy.

Without quoting further evidence, we can reasonably conclude that the reign of Elizabeth did not provide that background against which we would expect industry to progress, agriculture to flourish, or population to prosper.[17] It will be useful to bear this fact in mind when we come to estimate the number of inhabitants in the seventeenth century.

CR

We can get some information about the population of the county from the papers relating to the plantation of the north-east baronies, 1615-18. In the Commissioners' Return and Certificate "concerning the grievances of the Natives in the Plantation of Wexford," an outline is given of all the main features of that Plantation. This document would indicate that the number of inhabitants in the planted area was something over 15,000.

> "To the residue which claim to be freeholders, being for the most part possessed of but small portions, no allowance of land or recompense is assigned or given, but all they, in number 390 or thereabouts, and all the residue of the inhabitants, tenants, and cottiers, estimated to be 14,500 men, women and children, may be removed at the will of the patentees".[18]

The planted portion — consisting of the baronies of Gorey and Ballaghkeene and half Scarawalsh — represented about two-fifths the area of County Wexford. Accepting this figure of approximately 15,000 as a basis of calculation, it would be reasonable to conclude that the population of the County as a whole was at that time (1614) at something over 40,000. The figures given in the foregoing extract have been frequently quoted as evidence of the proportion of landowners in the total population; out of over 15,000 inhabitants not more than 667 claimed freeholds.[19]

A plantation of such magnitude must have caused a great deal of emigration, and hence led to a decline in the number of people living in these baronies. Information upon which we might base accurate conclusions is unfortunately not forthcoming; nevertheless, a paragraph in the State Papers, 1620, containing a reference to the transportation of some of the native Wexfordmen to Virginia helps to throw a little light on the emigration that took place at that time.[20] The Wexford freeholders had petitioned in 1616 against the plantation, and in a last desperate attempt to obtain justice, several hundred displaced landholders went to Dublin and urged their claims in person. These Wexfordmen — "men of the escheated countryies of Wexford, who have lately vexed their Lordships with their clamours against the distribution of the lands there" — were promptly thrown into prison, and some were sent to Virginia.[21] It was a period when British Colonial expansion in North America and the West Indies was at its height.

We have no information as to the exact number of Wexford people sent to Virginia at that time. There is reason, however, to believe that the number was considerable, as a result of research made by Irish-American scholars into the County Records by Virginia in the seventeenth century. In the Journals of the American-Irish Historical Society (notably Vol. XIII) some very interesting extracts are given from these Virginian Records, containing valuable lists of early colonists bearing Irish surnames. They include marriage registers and records of land grants. A perusal of these lists leaves no doubt that Wexford surnames are exceptionally well represented, a fact which would certainly support the view that emigration to Virginia from Wexford was by no means insignificant. Some of the names found in Virginia include Edmund Bolger, Garrett Brien, Richard Murphy, John Doyle, Henry Roche, Daniel Cavanegh, Edmund Murphy, Darby Byrne, Garret Byrne. A man called William Hutchin, the record tells, married a lady with that homely name, Nancy Cavanaugh. John Murphy was a witness to the will of Charles Cavenah of Edgecome County, which was probated in 1757.

Similarly in the records of the bordering State of North Carolina, Wexford surnames, particularly Murphy, are frequently found. In the first Census of that state (1790) no less than 72 heads of families had the name Murphy.[22] "In almost every parish register that has been preserved there is an entry of a Murphy," says Mr Michael J. O'Brien, who published some of these lists of names.

"The Murphys have been in North Carolina from an early date, and traces of people of this name can be found all over the Colony, from the City of Murfreesboro in Hertford County, in the eastern part of the State, to the town of Murphy, Cherokee County, in the extreme north-western part, on the border-line of Tennessee."

Colour is lent to the picture of Wexford emigration to Virginia and the West Indies by the presence here on the very borders of the confiscated baronies of an adventurous figure whose family is intimately associated with the colonisation of the West Indies. He was Lodowick Bryskett, a Londoner of Genoese parentage, who had come to Ireland in 1575 with Sir Henry Sidney as Clerk to the Privy Council.[23] He settled down near Enniscorthy and apparently looked after the affairs of that town for Wallop. In a letter written January 15, 1581, he announces his arrival here:

"The place which I have chosen is in the Countie of Wexford ... joyning upon the Duffrey and the Moroghes and neighboured by very quyett gentlemen of the Cavanaghs; but for situation very pleasant and the soyle very fertile. It was sometymes a Pryory belonging to the house of St John Jerusalem ... I pay £30 rent by the yere."

Later, when Wallop's garrison in Enniscorthy was assailed, he fled back to England. Three generations of the Bryskett family were to be closely associated with British Colonial expansion in the West Indies; in fact, Bryskett's son and grandson were the first Governors of Montserrat. Naturally his name comes to mind when we hear of the transportation of the dispossessed Wexfordmen to Virginia.[*]

---

[*] In one of the documents edited by Fr Gwynn (Analecta Hibernica, No. 4) there is an entry which provides a link between the Irish Catholic colonies of Virginia and Montserrat at this period. Under date January 26, 1634, the Latin Diary of Fr Andrew White says:

Having allowed for the uncertain nature of some of the evidence, the fact remains that County Wexford family names occur frequently in the early Virginian records. We can conclude that there was some emigration from the county to Virginia in the first half of the seventeenth century. Emigration was a feature of life here that was always in evidence throughout the century; it was undoubtedly an important factor in contributing to reduce still further the number of inhabitants.

C3

Assuming, then, that at the time of the Plantation the population of the county was in the neighbourhood of 40,000, and that this figure was reduced as a consequence of emigration, it is quite likely that the number of inhabitants increased in the third and fourth decades of the century; for the period prior to 1641 was marked by a degree of economic recovery, contrasting sharply with the destruction of the Elizabethan era that preceded it, and with the ravages of the Cromwellian era which followed it. By 1641, the population of Ireland had reached a peak figure judged by the standards of those times,[24] though Sir William Petty's estimate did not exceed one million and a half for the whole island. As early as 1612 we learn that Wexford and New Ross "being both corporate townes, are very populous of themselves and of much resort by strangers".[25] By 1641 Wexford was a port of

"Habet Monserrate incolas Hybernos pulsos ab Anglis Virginia ob fidei Catholicae professionem," and the English version of the same diary likewise records that in Montserrat "there is a noble plantation of Irish Catholique, whom the Virginians would not suffer to live with them on account of their religion" (p. 184). Amongst these Catholic inhabitants of Montserrat (where young Bryskett was Governor) were, perhaps, some of our own countymen, who had been transported to Virginia following the Plantation of James I, and were in turn banished from Virginia to Montserrat, because they remained loyal to the Faith of their forbears of Scarawalsh, Gorey and Ballaghkeene.

leading importance and the town was noted for the high proportion of Catholics amongst its people. A letter written later in the century describes the very large Catholic population there "in that city recently so wealthy" ("in ea tam nuper opulenta urbe").[26]

New Ross still retained something of its former greatness, having at one time held premier place amongst the great ports of Ireland. As early as the thirteenth century there had been a considerable population in the town. We are left in no doubt about this fact from the unusually detailed figures that are given in the celebrated poem written on the erection of the walls in 1265.[27] Despite the ebb and flow of its prosperity under the Tudors and early Stuarts, it was still a town of importance on the eve of the Cromwellian campaign, but the seventeenth century was to see a great part of its glory fade. In 1636, Robert Leigh tells us that an accidental fire burned down most of the town; over 300 slated houses were burned, besides many thatched houses. That the ancient prosperity of Ross had already been shattered is evident from this sentence in a letter written by Dr John Roche:

> "There is in my Diocese a famous city called New Ross, which aforetime surpassed most of the cities of Ireland in inhabitants and affluence of riches, now its early prosperity is visible only in its ruins."[28]

The occasional references to the town of Ferns at this period are invariably surrounded by a nostalgic glow, a reflection of an earlier glory that had by now all but vanished. "Ferns being but now a poor country village," Ram says in 1612, while some years later we are told, "The city of Ferns was once populous and important; it is now remarkable only for its antiquity, and its ruins scarcely preserve the traces of its former grandeur".[29]

છ

To whatever extent economic recovery had taken place up to 1641, it was now to be abruptly halted by the Confederate wars, and more so by the Cromwellian Campaign and subsequent Settlement. It is outside our scope in this article to deal with the history of these events; we are concerned merely with their effects on the size and distribution of the population of the county. Briefly, we may say that the effects on the population were disastrous, for before the Cromwellian epoch ended the traditional fabric of life had been mercilessly rent asunder. It would indeed be difficult to exaggerate the havoc wrought by the Cromwellian Campaign and Settlement. The extreme degree of misery to which the county had been reduced is evidenced by the fact that the figure for the total number of inhabitants in the Census of 1659[30] was as low as 13,680. The distribution of population of baronies, according to the Census, was:

Baronies	English	Irish	Total
Wexfford Towne and Liberties	340	562	902
New Ross Towne and Liberties	241	377	618
Enniscorthy Towne	67	322	389
Forth Barony	178	1,667	1,845
Bargie	126	1,353	1,479
Shelmaleer	163	1,650	1,813
Shelbryne	101	1,893	1,994
Bantry	56	1,347	1,403
Ballyaghkeene	122	1,219	1,341
Goary	107	687	794
Scarwelsh	131	971	1,102
	1,632	**12,048**	**13,680**

The student, it is true, may not accept these figures as entirely accurate. Nevertheless, it would be very rash to doubt the conclusion of Hardinge (who announced the discovery of this Census in the Transactions of the Royal

Irish Academy, 1864) that by about 1659 the population of the County was at its lowest point. The grounds for that conclusion are so overwhelming that they established the Cromwellian epoch as one of the great vital turning-points in our history. "Ireland, in the language of Scripture, now lay void as a wilderness," says John P. Prendergast. "Five-sixths of her people had perished. Women and children were found daily perishing in ditches, starved ... In the years 1652-3, the plague and famine had swept away whole counties, that a man might travel twenty or thirty miles and not see a living creature."[31] Every contemporary record depicts the scene as one of desolation and ruin. "The plight of the Irish race is terrible," wrote Dr French (18 November, 1651).[32] "After years of destructive warfare a stillness of death reigned over the Island," wrote the editor of the 1659 Census.

Nowhere is all this brought out with greater force than in the accounts of the terrible plight of the Catholic inhabitants of Wexford town. Out of the total population, we learn from Dr French's description, not 20 Catholics remained. As many as 6,000, we are told, were driven out to beg their bread, while the town was deprived of a still greater number of its citizens in other ways. Dr Luke Wadding says that of the large number of Catholics in the five parishes of the town, "scarcely 400 survived". [33] Writing in 1682 Solomon Richards tells us that Wexford town "was in good order and very populous since the last Rebellion, but much depopulated in its taking by Oliver Cromwell". Cromwell's message to the Speaker of the English Parliament seems to convey that Irish Military losses were not many less than 2,000; 300 people were drowned.

These accounts are sufficient to give us a general impression of the severe losses sustained here because the County had the misfortune to be in the direct path of the Cromwellian Sword. Losses due to the incidences of famine and pestilence were of no less importance. No part of the County remained immune from them. The Description of the Barony of Forth (written about 1680) says:

> "The Quartan Feaver since Cromwell's unsurpacion in
> that Barony (as elsewhere in the aforesaid county)
> much afflicted and destroyed many, its effects before
> being there hardlie mentioned, much less knowne." [34]

There was an outbreak of fever in New Ross after its capture by the Cromwellian forces. "During the winter of 1649-50," says Hore, "there was a dreadful epidemic of disease throughout all this neighbourhood. It was called the plague and decimated Ross." (*History of New Ross*, p.326). The north of the county did not escape from famine conditions, a fact which emerges from this entry in a letter sent in the Spring of 1653 to the Commissioners of Revenue at Wexford:

> "About Gorey, Enniscorthy and Arklow, the quantity
> of oxes expected out of these parts fall short of
> expectations, and many poor people are starved, and
> more are starving for want of corn." [35]

A factor of equal importance in reducing the population of the county was the banishment of the Catholic proprietors and the confiscation of their lands, as part of the great Cromwellian Plantation Plan. The care with which it was planned, and the thoroughness with which it was carried out, leave no doubt of its effect on the population. County Wexford was part of the territory (South of the Liffey and within the Barrow, known as the Five Counties) which was singled out for more thorough attention in the work of transplantation. On the 17 July, 1654, it was ordered that all the territory "should be wholly transplanted of Irish Papists by the 18 May, 1655, on pain of being taken as spies, and proceeded with before a Court Martial". Petitions were made against the order by Cromwellian officers who wished to employ some Irish on the land "which had long lain waste by the rebellion".[36] In addition to the emigration which arose directly from the transplantation scheme, the population suffered by the emigration that took place to the Continent during the same period.

Taking all the facts into consideration, it would be unreasonable to conclude that the population of the county in 1659 could have been much higher than the figure of 13,680 given in the Census. All the available testimony supports the view that the economic condition of the county was miserable, and that the number of inhabitants was at its lowest ebb.

The Northern Baronies were thinly populated comparative to the rest of the county, a fact which is evidenced by the Census figures, by the Parish Maps of the Down Survey, and by the Description of the County written by Robert Leigh in 1684.[37] In the greater part of these Baronies, the countryside was deserted and the soil had been little cultivated for a considerable time. Of one parish in Gorey Barony we are told (c.1655): "No house, or improvements thereon, but all waste," and of the Barony as a whole it is stated that "the soyle is generally arable, meadow and pasture, but of late years grown much over with Shrubs, Heath and Furz". The land in Ballaghkeene was also "much of late years overgrown with Furze and Heath".[38] The Barony of Forth succeeded in maintaining a comparatively high population, even after the ravages of the Cromwellian period had taken full toll of the county. This is clear from the same three contemporary sources. "The improvement thereof is so much," one Cromwellian Surveyor says of this Barony, "that there is not one parcell hardly without buildings, which are particularly described in the several parishes hereunto annexed". The details in the parish accounts leave us in no doubt about the point. The Description written about the year 1680 mentions that "the Barony is very populous, the villages nere one another and of narrow extent, hardly any farm contained 200 acres". Robert Leigh includes the Barony amongst the places in the county "best and thickest inhabited".

 C3

The Cromwellian authorities made strenuous efforts to clear all the towns of Ireland of their Catholic inhabitants; the consequence in many cases was to leave these towns in a ruinous state. An order issued by the Council, 4 March, 1657, from Dublin Castle, declared:

> "that all Popish recusants, as well proprietors as others, whose habitation is in any port-towns, walled-towns, or garrisons, and who did not before the 15 September, 1643 ... and ever since profess the Protestant Religion, should remove themselves and their families out of all such places, and two miles at the least distant therefrom, before 20 May next."[39]

It was found difficult to enforce strict compliance with the order, which had later to be renewed.

Colonel Sadleir (one of the Officers appointed to Superintend the Transplantation), when enforcing the other in Wexford town, sought specific answers to these queries:

> "Whether any Irish Papists shall be permitted to live in the town of Wexford? If any, whether all the Sea men, boatmen and fisherman or how many? How many packers and gillers of herrings? How many Coopers? How many Masons and Carpenters?" (Ibid. p. 119; also Hore, p. 311).

Together with the Catholics who, at the discretion of the local officers, were allowed to remain, many Catholics crept back. By 1682 Solomon Richards could say of Wexford town:

> "The greatest number of the inhabitants are Irish — but the Magistracy are all English or Protestant."

Two years later Robert Leigh tells us of New Ross:

> "The inhabitants are for the most part ancient natives of the towne and countrye about it, and soe are the

chiefe merchants there that trade beyond seas, but those that have the Government of the Corporation and all publique employments there are Engiish of a late standing."[40]

In 1695 nine-tenths of the sea-faring men in Wexford and New Ross were Catholics. [41]

The three decades between the Restoration and the Revolution gave some opportunity for economic recovery. Sir William Petty's estimate of the population of Ireland in 1672 was 1,300,000. Gradually the countryside came to be repopulated, and the towns began to regain their prosperity. But the process in this country was a slow one. At the time of Dr French's death (1678), Dr Luke Wadding says that "in his poor Diocese, or throughout Catholic Ireland, there are no longer Country Houses in which a wandering Prelate could be concealed or protected". As late as 1684 the ancient prosperity of New Ross had been so little restored that the town contained in that year only "150 stone houses, slated, and about as many thatched ones". Leigh's account goes on:

> "Ross has pretty good trading for wine and fruits oute of Spaine and France, and alsoe for transporting of Beefe, hydes, and tallow; but not above one halfe of the ground within the walls is built upon and many even of those buildings ruinated."

Of Bannow, he says:

> "The town of Bannow is now quite ruined — there being nothing there but the ruins of an Old Church, of several stone houses, and ancient streets, of some few cabins, yet it sends two Burgesses to Parliament,"

and speaking of Clonmines, he remarks that it is:

"a very ancient Corporation, but now quite ruinated
... yet it sends two Burgesses to Parliament still."[+] [42]

It was in the seventeenth century that Enniscorthy began
to develop into an important town. Previous to this it is often
described as a mere hamlet. Its rise is intimately bound up
with the extensive forests that adjoin the town to the north
and west. Sir William Brereton informs us that "the greatest
part of all the wealthy inhabitants of the town (there cannot
be many) are wood-merchants". This was in 1635. Eighteen
years earlier Fr Donat Mooney brings out the same point in
his description of the Franciscan Convent, when he speaks of
the many products of the woods which were transported
down the Slaney to Wexford. [43] Wallop had not neglected to
use this opportunity of enriching himself by claiming as
customs the thirteenth-part of all the timber passing through
the town. [44] Later in the century extensive use was being
made of these forests in connection with the important
ironworks which had grown up in the neighbourhood.
"There are now two considerable ironworks belonging to this
towne," says Robert Leigh in 1684, "which is the reason why
it is well inhabited". Earlier Colonel Robert Phayre was
engaged in the manufacture of sword-blades in the village of
Forge. In 1661 the ironworks at Enniscorthy is again
mentioned and we are told that expenses were incurred "in
bringing over many hundred English workmen and their
families" (CSPI 1660-2, p.474). There are numerous other

[+] Leigh says of Taghmon that, although it sends two Burgesses to
Parliament, "it is now quite waste in a manner, there being there but
a ruinous old Castle, and a small parish church in repaire, and
about a dozen cabbins, and ye ruins of the aforesaid Chappels".
Fethard has 30 or 40 cabins, he says, together with three small
castles, a large parish Church, now unroofed, and a stone house and
a Brick house (built by Mr Loftus). "There is a convenient Creek for
fishermen at Fethard, but noe key, yet they make good use of it and
take good sea fish thereabouts."

contemporary references to these ironworks and to the forests in the neighbourhood.[45] From the woods the town derived its main source of wealth; to the trees it owed its growth.

Of the density and distribution of the population in the county towards the end of the century, we learn from Leigh's description of County Wexford in 1684:

> "This County (or moste parte of it) lyes in ye Dioses of Fearnes ... and is but thinly inhabited. The Baronys of Forth, Bargy, Shelmaleere and Shelburne and by the sea side about Arclow and Gorey are the places best and thickest inhabited."

That places near the sea-coast were more densely peopled can also be shown from the Census of 1659.[46] Throughout the century very large numbers of men depended for their livelihood on fishing, and there is no lack of evidence to show that fishing was an industry of primary importance in the seventeenth century. [47] In 1695 there were 346 fishermen in Wexford Town (amongst the 426 sea-faring men there); in New Ross there were 182 sea-faring men, of whom 85 were fishermen. [48] A fine trade in provisions had been built up; in the agricultural economy of the county, pasture was dominant. The experience of the first half of the century was unlikely to encourage tillage; it is easy to understand the reluctance to sow where the stranger might reap. We know from Leigh's account that the potato formed an important part of the food of the poorer sections of the people, although in other parts of Ireland it did not become the popular food till the eighteenth century. [49]

In the end of the eighteenth century we find the name of the Insurgent leader, William Barker, associated with these Ironworks. In 1796, he had leased from John Wheeler Pounden "the lands, garden, houses and concerns, called and known by the name of the Foundry in the Town of Enniscorthy, and all the Buildings and Improvements erected and made thereon, together with the use of the Watercourse which runs by and through the same".

ଔ

It is difficult to separate local history from national history, and inevitably the story of Wexford merges into the story of Ireland. Here, as elsewhere in Ireland, the extremely disturbed conditions of the century had impeded economic development. "Three times in the course of a single century, the orderly and normal economic progress of Ireland was interrupted by political cataclysms." [50] The aftermath of the Williamite War, the new confiscations, the Penal Laws, the destruction of the woollen trade, had caused a great flow of emigration, with a consequent diminution in the number of inhabitants. It was Lecky's opinion that the population of Ireland in 1700 was not far from two millions. [51]

County Wexford had escaped none of those calamities which had contributed to leave the population of Ireland at such a low ebb. The county had, in fact, endured more than its share of the dire results of war and famine and plantation. It is no exaggeration to say that a land of smiling plenty had been transformed into a desolate waste. It is not surprising, therefore, that the population of the county at the end of the century was at a low level. It could not have been more than half the present-day figure. What is surprising is the fact that the old Catholic families of the county still formed the great majority of its inhabitants. [52]

Fused into the consciousness of a common nationality, under pressure of religious persecution early in the century; these families — Gaedheal and Norman — endured together the trials and struggles of that century, and at its close, still made up the greater part of the county's population. Through so many changes, the country folk of the old nation had clung tenaciously to their ancestral territories, although the power and wealth of the county lay in other hands. Their heroic devotion to Faith and Home brings out the truth of the words written by David Rothe, Bishop of Ossory, early in the century, concerning the Wexfordmen who had lost their lands in the Plantation of James I:

"It is their nature," he wrote,

"that they would rather feast on husks at home that feast richly anywhere else, and they will fight for their altars and hearths, and seek a bloody death near the graves of their fathers, rather than be buried as exiles in foreign earth and alien sands."[53]

CR

[1]Census of Ireland, 1841.

[2]Transactions RIA Vol. 3 (1789-90). "An Essay Towards Ascertaining the Population of Ireland" —Gervase Parke Bushe.

[3](a) Edward Hay: *History of Insurrection of Co. Wexford, 1798* — Introduction and Appendices; (b) JKL: *Letters on the State of Ireland, 1825*, p. 98.

(c) *Fraser's Statistical Survey* (1807) for information on number of inhabitants per house in Wexford Town.

A recent work — *The Population of Ireland, 1750-1845* (K. M. Connell) would suggest that Bushe's estimates were too high, but this opinion, in so far as it concerns County Wexford, is not supported by local evidence.

[4]Census of Ireland, 1821.

[5]Census of Ireland, 1851 and 1861.

[6]The number of emigrants from the County between 1851 (1 May) and 1861 (31 March) was 27,053 (Census of 1911, County Wexford, p. 143).

[7]*Early Irish Laws and Institutions*, p. 37.

[8]*Journal of Statistical and Social Enquiry Society of Ireland,* (1936).

[9]*History of the Town and County of Wexford* (P. H. Hore), p. 235. Quoting Cal. S. P. Hen. VIII, 1520.

[10]Ibid. p. 247.

[11]*Pestilentia Magna per Wexfordiam, Dublin, Naas, Athie ac Leighlin — Pontem* (Annals: Dowling: Irish Archaeological Society).

[12]*Hore's New Ross*, p. 249.

[13]Hore: vi. 401.

[14]Annála Ríogaita Éireann, 1580: — "Tángattar Caománaig Agur Cennrelaig, Branaig Agur Tuaialaig … A ccobair Agur a ccommbáró Shemair lurtar Gur bó h-aen clár impearna Agur eraonta Ó Sláine co Sionainn, Agur Ó Dóinn co Comar Trí n-Uirce."

[15]Hore: vi.

[16] Ibid.

[17]Cf: *The Making of Ireland and its Undoing* (Alice Stopford Green) for an account of the condition of Ireland at the end of the Elizabethan Wars: "Of the flourishing markets and fair towns of the Irish, nothing was left but a starving village, a dim tradition, a crumbling wall, or the name of a silent meadow, while the ports lay empty, and rivers and lakes deserted." (p. 234).

[18]Hickson: *Ireland in the 17th century*, Vol. I, Appendix B.

[19]Dr George O'Brien: *Economic History of Ireland in the 17th century*, p. 34; Butler: *Policy of Surrender and Regrant*, p. 103.

[20]Analecta Hibernica, No. 4 (1932): *Documents Relating to the Irish in the West Indies*; collected and edited by Rev. Aubrey Gwynn, SJ, MA: The subject of Wexford emigration to Virginia was fully dealt with by Fr Gwynn in *Studies* (1929) — *Early Irish Emigration to the West Indies*.

[21]Cal. S. P. Ireland, 8 December, 1620. Full Text in Analecta Hibernica No. 4, p. 159.

[22]Journal American-Irish Historical Society, Vol. XIV.

[23]*Life and Correspondence of Lodowick Bryskett*. By Henry R. Polmer and Tom Peete Cross (University of Chicago Press, 1927).

[24]Transactions RIA, 1864. Article by Hardinge.

[25]Hore: vi. 261.

[26]Commentarius Rinuccinianus: Vol. IV., p. 298.

[27]Hore: Ross, p. 59. In Patrick Donovan's fine contribution to our local history, *The Story of Ross* (*The People* newspapers, 1946-7) the author says: "The trade of Ross port at its peak years is inconsistent with any but a very large population." He estimates the town's population at not less than 10,000 during that period.

[28]Hore: vi., p. 316.

[29]Ibid., p. 313.

[30]*A Census of Ireland* (c. 1659): Ed. Seamus Pender, M.A. (Irish Manuscripts Commission).

[31]*Cromwellian Settlement of Ireland* (John P. Prendergast), p. 307.

[32]*Spicilegium Ossoriense*, Vol. 2, p. 97.

[33]Hore, VI., p. 324: Notes Towards a Parochial History of the Diocese of Ferns (Dr Granntan Flood), p. xvi.

[34]Description of the Barony of Forth (c. 1680): Kilkenny and SE of Ireland Antiquarian Society, 1862.

[35]Dunlop: *Ireland Under the Commonwealth*, Vol. 2, p. 329.

[36]*Cromwellian Settlement of Ireland* (Prendergast), p. 269-70.

[37]Robert Leigh of Rosergarland: *Account of the Southern Part of Co Wexford, 1684*: (Kilkenny Archaeological Journal, 1858).

[38]Descriptive particulars accompanying Parish Maps of Down Survey. Copies in National Library of Ireland.

[39]*Cromwellian Settlement of Ireland*, p. 284.

[40]*Hore: History of Ross*, p. 369.

[41]*Arthur Young's Tour in Ireland.*

[42]Robert Leigh says of Ballyhack: "It is a sad place to look upon and has not above halfe a dozen houses and old pile of a Castle, besides a fue cabbins." At Old Ross he found "a large 'ould Castle which is quite out of repaire, where there is also an 'ould ruined Church, and about 50 cabbins of thatched houses." He records that in that year "Mr Loftus was building a key fishing boats ... neare a place called ye Slade."

[43]Analecta Hibernica, No. 6.

[44]Hore: vi.

[45](a) *Journal of Thomas Dinely: Giving Some Account of his Visit to Ireland in the Reign of Charles II. (Cork Historical and Archaeological Society Journal)*;

(b) Also Description of Parish of Templeshanbo, Down Survey Parish Maps;

(c) *Travels of Sir William Brereton* (C. Litton Falkiner: Illustrations of Irish History);

(d) *Abdy Letters* (Mss. In Nat. Lib.).

[46]*The Past* (Organ of the Ui Ceinnsealaigh Historical Society), 1948, p. 112.

---

[47]*Travels of Sir William Brereton.* See also Solomon Richards' *Account of the Barony of Forth*; and George Griffith's *Chronicles of Co. Wexford*, p. 53.

[48]Arthur Young's Tour.

[49]"Ye great support of ye poore sortes of people is thire potatos which are much used all over the County."

[50]*Economic History of Ireland in the 17th century* (O'Brien).

[51]*History of Ireland in the 18th century.* Vol. I.

[52]Chronicles of the County Wexford, (George Griffiths), p. 6.

[53]*Analecta Sacra de Rebus Catholicorum in Hibernia*, 1617, p. 159 (David Rothe, Bishop of Ossory). Quoted in translation from *Ireland: A Documentary Record, 1607-1782.* Complied and edited by James Carthy.

Bishop Rothe in that work devoted several pages to the Plantation of North Wexford. He praises highly the dispossessed landholders, their mental alertness and physical prowess ("Tam ardua mente et robusto corpore"). Pointing out that they were entirely dependent on the land of their livelihood, he gives us a glimpse at the agricultural economy of the confiscated districts — "Nullis opibus instructos, praeter pauca armenta et iumenta; nulla industria praeditos, praeter agriculturam et pasturam pecorum." The planted area was well populated before the Plantation; the inhabitants, he says, were "multa prole oneratos", and again, "tametsi inermes, tamen agmine numeros" (p.158). He gives the extent of the planted area as follows: "territoria quae continent tres fere Baronias, iugera terrae arabilis 66,800 praeter sylvas, paludes, et sterillia montana" (p. 232: Dr Moran's Edition).

ଔ

THE COLCLOUGHS OF TINTERN
ABBEY AND DUFFRY HALL

God, full of mercy, pow'r
  and might,
Save or we perish in tempest
  to-night,
For His sake, Who uttered
  the glad words to save
His ship and His servants
  on Galilee's wave,
Oh save, and I will build to
  Thy glory alone
An altar of gold
  in an abbey of stone.
An abbey and altar,
  a church and a shrine,
This heart's grateful offering
  to mercy divine.

— John Bowers.

The Cistercian Abbey of Tintern, on the western side of
Bannow Lough, was built in 1200. Its founder was the
Norman lord, William Marshall, who had married
Strongbow's daughter Isabella. He was on a voyage between
Milford and Waterford when a tempest arose at sea and he
found himself in imminent peril. He made a vow to found an
abbey in that place where, with God's help, he should safely

land. The ship landed in safety on Bannow Lough. Without delay he set about fulfilling his vow. He brought over Cistercian monks from Tintern Abbey in Monmouthshire, gave them spacious lands and ample liberties and called his new monastery "Little Tintern" or "Tintern Minor". It was also named "Tintern de Voto" (of the vow).

The famous Tintern Abbey in Wales was built on the right bank of the river Wye about ten miles south of the town of Monmouth. The Wexford Tintern was dedicated in its entirety to the Blessed Virgin Mary. Dunbrody Abbey, a short distance away, had been erected in 1175. These two religious houses flourished for almost four hundred years and forged during those medieval centuries a glorious link between Wexford and the great Order of St Bernard of Clairvaux.

> "Tintern Abbey in Wexford like its sister Abbey in Monmouthshire appears to have been singularly beautiful and rich in sculptured monuments,"

says a modern scholar.

> "As in the English abbey, the ruins of our abbey abound with beautifully sculptured figures representing the saints."

Though their family name has been long and closely associated with Tintern Abbey, the Colcloughs cannot be numbered amongst the early Norman families of Wexford. The foundation of the Cistercian Abbey, and the coming of the old Norman families date from the twelfth century, but it was not until the middle of the sixteenth century that the Colcloughs first came to the county.

At the time of the Dissolution of the Monasteries by Henry VIII, Tintern Abbey with its lands was taken over and granted to Sir Anthony Colclough. Coming of a Staffordshire family, he was then serving with the Royal forces in Ireland. The grant was a reward for his services in furthering the king's cause against the native Irish families. That part of the abbey which had been the domicile of the monks was transformed into a family dwelling-house. "The erection of this residence," says Philip Hore, "has totally destroyed the most inspiring and beautiful portion of the ruins."

Through Sir Anthony Colclough the Tintern interest continued for three hundred years in the male line until, about the middle of the last century, it passed to the female line. John Thomas Rosborough assumed his wife's family name when he married Mary Colclough. She was daughter of Cæsar Colclough, who became Chief Justice of Prince Edward Island.

During these three centuries the Colcloughs played a notable part in the public life of County Wexford. The family spread itself widely over various parts of the county and gathered influence and power. At times members of the family found themselves in popular favour and esteem because they were prominent in espousing the cause of the people amongst whom they lived.

A traveller through Ireland in 1752 described Tintern as follows:

> "I came to the old Convent of Tintern, turned into a mansion house of the Colcloughs. The church was large, with a great tower in the middle; the Chancel part was converted into a house with three floors and chimneys, of which I never saw an instance before. I was informed that this family came over in Queen Elizabeth's time, and that an ancestor, marrying a Papist, went over to the Papist religion."

He added that the Colcloughs had at that time established a spinning school and linen factory and built a little market house in the village.

For a proper understanding of the history of this county it is useful to get a clear idea of the background of the Colcloughs. They figured so prominently in the life of the county that their story is a long one indeed, especially as active members of the Grand Jury, and as representatives in the Irish Parliament for the numerous "Pocket boroughs" in County Wexford. The Colcloughs were prominent in the activities of Grattan's Volunteers. Sir Vesey Colclough was one of the leaders who attended the county meeting of the Volunteers held at The Bear Inn, Enniscorthy, on March 8, 1782. The meeting was held to endorse the famous resolutions passed at the Dungannon Convention in the previous month, at a time when a healthy spirit of goodwill and tolerance prevailed in the county.

The best-known Wexfordman who bore the surname was John Henry Colclough who took part in the 1798 Rising. He lived at Ballyteigue Castle, Kilmore. With Bagenal Harvey, he was arrested on the Great Saltee Island, was court-martialled for his part in the Rising, and hanged on Wexford Bridge on June 28, 1798. At the time of the Penal Laws, Dudley Colclough of Mohurry acted as surety for many "registered" priests in the Diocese of Ferns in 1704, under the "Act for Registering the Popish Clergy" (see appendix to Dr W. H. Grattan Flood's *Notes for a History of the Diocese of Ferns*).

Dudley Colclough lived at Duffry Hall, Kiltealy, which was a flourishing residence of the Duffry branch of the Colcloughs. Sir Thomas Colclough, son of Sir Anthony, was the first of the surname to establish himself in the Duffry territory. The word Duffry is derived from the Irish word *Duibhthir* (black country). Almost entirely covered with forest, the Duffry country extended from Enniscorthy to Mount Leinster. That is the origin of Enniscorthy's Duffry Gate — it was the entrance to the town from the wooded area between the Urrin and the Glesha.

It is difficult to define accurately the boundaries of the Duffry because they varied from time to time. Early in the reign of James I, Sir Thomas acquired some land in the Duffry, and gradually the Colclough estates there grew in extent, partly by private purchase, partly by State grant. We are told that the property held by Sir Thomas included "the Castle, town and lands of Monart".

In December, 1685, Patrick Colclough got a grant of forty townlands in the Duffry to hold forever at a yearly rent of £60. The area was estimated at 7,800 acres. Thirty years before this, the family had suffered very heavy losses during the Cromwellian Plantation. At that time those of the Colcloughs who were Protestants were left in undisturbed possession, while those who were Catholics lost their property. Amongst the latter was Dudley Colclough, who forfeited 1,600 acres in Moyacork parish, including Garryhasten; 12,000 acres in Templeshanbo parish, including Monart; and 800 acres in St John's parish, Barony of Shelmalier. He is described as Dudley Colclough of Mohurry and Monart. He was ordered in 1653 to transplant to Connacht but was granted three months to gather together the remains of his harvest and stock and to cut down £100 worth of timber, which he sold to Francis Harvey, merchant, of Wexford. Later Dudley's son, Patrick, obtained about half of this forfeited acreage. Patrick was MP for Wexford County in James II's Parliament of 1689.

It is probable that the mansion at Duffry Hall was built at the time that Patrick Colclough was granted forty townlands. It enjoyed the full height of its splendour in the middle of the eighteenth century. It was intended originally as a dower house for Tintern, a place where the heir of Tintern lived while he waited to come into his inheritance. It is clear that later Duffry Hall was the separate residence of the Duffry or Mohurry branch of the family. It was then described as a "fine massive mansion with ample accommodation for a large family, besides a great number of guests with their servants and attendants". The deerpark at Duffry Hall was so extensive that it stretched right to the top of the mountain. When Colclough of Duffry Hall mortgaged his lands, he mortgaged half a barony. Extending as far as Galbally and Garrenstackle, his lands stretched northward beyond Ryland and Glasslacken.

Patrick Colclough of Mohurry was granted a licence in 1685 to hold a weekly market on Tuesday, and two fairs annually on August 15 and October 27. There are numerous leases extant executed by Cæsar Colclough in the subsequent decades referring to places like Curraduff. He is described as "Cæsar Colclough of Duffry Hall and Tintern". He was born in 1694. He married Henriette Vesey of Lucan — this is where the name *Vesey* comes into the family. When he died in 1766, he had completed a term of 43 years as Portreeve (chief citizen) of the Corporation of the town of Enniscorthy.

Throughout the eighteenth century the Colcloughs dominated the Borough of Enniscorthy, until March 1800 when the Tintern branch disposed of it for £13,000 to Lord Lismore. The will of Dudley Colclough of Mohurry dated 1722 was printed in *The Past* (vol. 2). By it he bequeathed three pounds to the parish priest of Templeshanbo and Enniscorthy. "I will bequeath unto Michael Fitzhenry, my parish priest, the sum of three pounds sterling to be paid him at my decease and also that he shall hold and enjoy the lands of Shroughmore now in his possession during his life rent free." He bequeathed one pound each to the Catholic clergy of the diocese of Ferns.

The greater part of the Duffry estates of the Colcloughs was wooded. On one occasion after the Restoration, the proprietors of the Enniscorthy Ironworks disputed their right to full ownership of the forests, as distinct from the lands, but the Colcloughs had influence enough to have a special Act passed by the Irish Parliament confirming their right to the woods. As late as 1811 Duffry Hall is shown clearly on Valentine Gill's *Map of Co. Wexford* in all its delightful sylvan setting.

The exploits on the hurling field of the lords of Duffry Hall are well-known. The Colclough name became a household word in many parts of Ireland for their skill at the craft of the camán. The story is told that Adam Colclough of Duffry Hall had seven sons. Two teams were chosen from the best hurling talent in the country. Three sons played with one team and three with the other. The game was played on the famous lawn at Duffry Hall and an old tradition relates that the seventh brother, mounted on a splendid hunter, threw in the ball and then presided as judge, or referee.

In the books of Patrick Kennedy there are numerous references to Duffry Hall, and in *Evenings in the Duffry*, he says:

> "I would not desire a pleasanter occupation on a fine morning than a walk through Killoughrim and Moynart Wood, past Duffry Hall, and up the Gap of Scollagh, with glimpses of Black Stairs on the left and Mount Leinster on the right, marking the variety formed by the grey rocks and purple heath above, and the green patches lying like islands among them."

The great folklorist in the same book quotes many verses in praise of the Colcloughs. Speaking of a rival landlord who was about to become their adversary in a legal battle, one verse says:

> *"Can he compare his bogs and*
> *heaths to the woods of*
> *Moghurry*
> *Where the bugles were a-sounding,*
> *and the huntsmen a-running?*
> *He thinks himself a lord when he*
> *kills a black-nosed sheep,*
> *While three ox-beefs are slaughtered*
> *in Moghurry every week."*

In Kennedy's chapter, *A Day at Duffry Hall*, one of the characters says of the Colcloughs:

> "I do not remember to have ever heard of a tyrannical thing done by the family, and I have heard of numbers of kind and generous ones."

George Griffths, Editor of *The Watchman* (Enniscorthy), wrote a good article in 1877 on the Colcloughs of Tintern, in which he briefly relates the well-known story of the rise of the village of Saltmills. "The last Cæsar Colclough who dwelt in Tintern," says Griffiths, "had a dislike to have 'cabins' so near him, and the old village of Tintern was pulled down and Saltmills arose."

Kennedy in *Evenings in the Duffry* was recording faithfully the tradition of the district. The whole story is an excellent illustration of the truth of G. K. Chesterton's dictum that, while tradition may on occasions miss the facts, it never misses the point. And the point in this instance is that the Colcloughs of Duffry Hall had won for themselves a special place in the affections of the people. Another verse quoted by Patrick Kennedy puts it this way:

> *"Now may out Duffry heroes and*
> *the Yellow Bellies all*
> *For ever beat the Wicklow boys*
> *in hurling and football:*
> *May Jones of Achasallach be*
> *banished over say,*
> *And Colclough reign at Duffry*
> *Hall for ever and a day."*

ଔ

TUSKAR LIGHTHOUSE

In the grey of the coming
on of a night
She dropped the tug
at the Tuskar Light
And the topsails went
to the topmost head
To a chorus that fairly
awoke the dead

— John Mansfield.

The erection of Tuskar Lighthouse was completed in 1815. The lighthouse at Hook Head is centuries older. As early as 1657 the description of The Hook parish in the Down Survey says:

"This parish is a point and runs far into the sea, on the furthermost part of which stands a Tower, which formerly hath been a Lighthouse to conduct ships into ye harbour."

The place-name Tuskar is said to be of Norse origin. The rock lies about seven miles off the Wexford coast, nearly due east between Carnsore Point and the Greenore Point. Its location is 52° 12' N. Lat. and 6° 12' W. Long. The rock is about 300 feet in length, 150 feet in breadth and its most elevated part is 30 feet above the level of the sea at high-water mark. It meets the tremendous unbroken surge of the Atlantic bearing up the Channel and, though the summit is raised considerably above the level of the tide, it is constantly submerged in the wintry gales. A gazetteer of the last century speaks of the Tuskar as consisting of "four masses of rock arranged in a line from North to South, called Tuskar, the North Hen and Chickens, and the South Hen and Chickens, and all lying within a space of two furlongs from extremity to extremity".

For many centuries before the advent of steam this part of the Wexford coast was the scene of many great shipping disasters. Vessels were wrecked on this treacherous coast where there was no shelter from the prevailing south-west winds. As Philip Hore wrote:

> "The eddies and currents between the Saltees and the land, and around Carnsore Point were discovered only after some sad experiences by sailors whose vessels by confused seas were driven out of their course and wrecked either on the Saltees, or the Connigs, Brandis and Barrel Rocks, or on the forbidding coast itself,"

He added that the people of Carne district, till the close of the eighteenth century, derived much of their wealth from the frequent shipwrecks that occurred on these dangerous coasts, "until the erection of the Lighthouse on Tuskar Rock put an end to these dreadful occurrences".

A Stanza from the sea-ballad *The Glasgow*, illustrates the point simply and well:

> *"Early the following morning,*
> *about half past four o'clock*
> *Our gallant ship with all her might*
> *come on the sunken rock*
> *These rocks are called "The Barrels,"*
> *They're hidden from human sight;*
> *They lie abreast of Carne*
> *and west of Tuskar light."*

The first reference I can find to any proposal for the erection of a lighthouse on Tuskar is in a letter preserved in the State Paper Office in Dublin. It is a petition from Sir Hugh Palliser to the Lords of the Treasury "for a grant of the rock for the purpose of erecting a Beacon or Lighthouse". It is dated July 14, 1800. Before replying to this petition, the Treasury took steps to obtain information on the matter in Co Wexford. Meanwhile, a letter from Mr R. A. Annesley on August 19 stated that "the erection of a lighthouse on that rock would be a public advantage". Three days later, Marsden of the Chief Secretary's office established the fact, from information received through Thomas Richards of Wexford, "that the Tuskar Rock has not ever been claimed as part of any estate on the adjoining coast" who presumed the property belonged to the Lords of the Admiralty.

Due, no doubt, to the Napoleonic Wars, there is little further reference to the proposal till 1811, when the Ballast Board wrote to the Lord Lieutenant stating that it was their opinion "that a lighthouse ought to be built on Tuskar Rock as the best position for a sea-light on that part of the coast". The board received a memorial from Waterford Chamber of Commerce against the proposal on the grounds that the Saltee Islands would be a better position. The matter was decided in favour of Tuskar by January, 1812, and work was soon commenced on the erection of a lighthouse on a plan prepared by a man called George Halpin; the work was carried out under his direction by workmen of the Ballast Board. Horizontal beams, firmly held by iron clamps, were first laid across the rock. Temporary workshops were built, and huts capable of sheltering forty-one workmen.

The huts had scarcely been erected when a ship from the West Indies was wrecked on the base of the rock. The ship was bound for Liverpool and had 107 passengers on board. The night was dark and all the people on board would have lost their lives but for the help received from the workmen who, using ropes, raised them to the summit and saved them all except four.

But a much greater disaster was soon to follow. During the month of October, strong gales from the south-west swept over the rock, culminating in a violent tempest on Sunday, October 18. Huge billows rolled over Tuskar. An unusually high tide occurred. Some of the men ran from their huts to the highest point of the rock, but before the rest could escape, a sudden surge of the sea swept the huts and their occupants away.

A contemporary account speaks of men being buried beneath the moving mountains of water. The men at the summit clung at the rock for several days while the waves beat over them. Fourteen men lost their lives, but some accounts say the figure was as high as thirty. The survivors were later brought to Wexford in a state of extreme exhaustion. On the same night the "Smalls" Lighthouse, near Landsend, was almost entirely destroyed.

All the sheds and huts on the rock were swept away. The Board made generous provision for the dependants of the men who were killed. The terrible disaster, we are told, made a deep impression on the minds of the people in the neighbourhood and no offers could induce the workmen again to approach the rock. After some time, the Board in charge of Irish Lighthouses decided to undertake the work once again. Smeaton's plans of the famous Eddystone Lighthouse were taken as a model. Eddystone is off Plymouth in the English Channel. Stones were raised from the rocks near Dublin and the materials of the new lighthouse were fitted there. They were then conveyed from Dublin to Tuskar, and in about eighteen months the work was completed, at the cost of over £30,000.

The lighthouse was a circular building made of Dublin granite, painted white. The light was 105 feet above sea-level; it was revolved every two minutes; its flash was visible every ten seconds and the bright light could be seen at a distance of fifteen miles in clear weather. During foggy weather, a bell was tolled by machinery every half-minute. Many writers have lavished praise on the wonderful service rendered by

Tuskar Lighthouse to seamen, especially with the increasing mercantile coastal traffic in the Channel.

THE EDDYSTONE OF IRELAND

The Parliamentary Gazette of 1846 says that "Tuskar Lighthouse is one of the most valuable works ever constructed on the Irish coast". Mrs Hall says that "the entire construction is a fine work of art and though the furious billows have beaten to a height of fifty feet on the cone-shaped building, not the least effect or injury has been suffered".

"The importance and exposure of its situation," says Philip Hore, "the arduous difficulty of erecting an edifice on it, and the dreadful accidents to which such an attempt has been liable, all combine to render this rock the Eddystone of Ireland." The author of the sea-ballad, *The Lofty Caravaille*, a French shipwrecked on the Blackwater sand-banks refers to "Tuskar's grand revolving light".

> *"Yet their case was now no better*
> *For her steerage broke away,*
> *And Boreas blew with vengeance*
> *Until the break of day.*
> *And at the glimpse of daylight,*
> *Blackwater Tower they see,*
> *And Tuskar's grand revolving light*
> *They had it in their lee."*

Let us briefly list, in conclusion, the lightships which mark dangers of the Wexford coast:

(1) Arklow — About eight miles from Courtown Harbour. Moored about two miles to the south of Arklow Bank. Exhibits a white light, giving two flashes every forty-five seconds.

(2) Blackwater — About 8 miles eastward from Blackwater Head. Moored about three miles to the

east of Blackwater Bank. Exhibits a white flashing light, one flash every fifteen seconds.

(3) Barrels — About four miles form Carnsore Point. Moored about two miles south of Barrels Rock. A red flashing light, two flashes every thirty seconds.

(4) Coningbeg — About eight miles from Kilmore. Moored about two miles to the south of Coninbeg Rock. A white light, three flashes every minute.

[The first three of these have since gone. The Blackwater Lightship was taken out of action in 1968 — Editor].

Mrs Hall describes Tuskar light as "the mariner's guiding star to the Irish Channel". In our day the light is used by air pilots to check their course. The light of Tuskar can be seen on high ground in many parts of Wexford, as far west as Scollagh Gap. Hosts of Wexford folk, winter and summer, especially along the coast, have a warm welcome for this friendly, familiar flash.

Tuskar light was first seen on June 4, 1815, exactly a fortnight before the Battle of Waterloo was fought.

ଔ

ENNISCORTHY, VIRGINIA, USA

Since the middle of the eighteenth century there has been a centre in Virginia, USA, called Enniscorthy. It was founded by a man called John Coles and was named by him "Enniscorthy" after his ancestral home in Enniscorthy, County Wexford.

It is situated on the Green Mountain, a charming eminence, heavily wooded, where a river breaks a passage through the hills in Albemarle, County Virginia. Enniscorthy was built on this delightful hill, with a sweeping view of the horizon to the south-east and the Black Ridge Mountains in the west.

County Wexford had an earlier link with Virginia, when at the time of the Plantation of North Wexford, many of the landholders were sent to the Virginian colony. The Wexford freeholders — men from the Baronies of Gorey and Ballaghkeene and Scarawalsh — had petitioned in 1616 against the Plantation, and in a last desperate attempt to get justice, several hundred of them went to Dublin and urged their claims in person. These Wexfordmen — "men of the escheated countryies of Wexford who have lately vewed their lordships with their clamours against the distribution of the lands there" — were promptly thrown into prison and some were sent to Virginia. Wexford surnames are well represented in the early records of that state, in land grants and marriage registers.

John Coles emigrated from his home town of Enniscorthy to Virginia, USA, early in the eighteenth century. By 1747 he had already become a wealthy merchant and landowner at Richmond and in that year he established a very large estate and residence on a tract of 6,500 acres patented by a man called Francis Epps in 1730. He named the place *Enniscorthy* and it became the permanent home of the Coles family. A writer on Virginian life of those days says that "*Enniscorthy* was then the centre of hospitable social life on the Green Mountains".

John Coles bequeathed Enniscorthy to his son John, who became a prominent figure in the public life of Virginia. He was a prosperous, widely-known agriculturist and married Elizabeth Tucker of Norfolk. He was on terms of intimate friendship with many of the great figures of the American Independence movement. His son, a barrister, later became President Jefferson's confidential secretary and a Colonel in the War of 1812. The daughters of John Coles married into leading Virginian families like the Rutherfolds and Stevensons.

One daughter was Mrs Sallie Coles Stevenson, wife of the United States Minister in London about 1840. Her letters to her sister, Mrs Rutherford, have recently been published in book form. This Sarah Coles was born at Enniscorthy, Virginia, the same week in which George Washington took office as the first President of the United States. While she was living in London, Enniscorthy was destroyed by fire. It was then described as "one of the most extensive and commodious residences in the State of Virginia". Colonel Coles died in 1841 and in 1850 his widow rebuilt Enniscorthy, which subsequently passed out of the hands of the Coles family.

A recent description of the place says:

"The main portion of the present house is built of brick with porches and entrances on both the east and west wings, and a rear entrance on the north. Enniscorthy, in the midst of the true beauty of Albemarle, still stands with the dignity of its age. The garden is still sweet and charming and seems to join in the peaceful quiet of the Coles graveyard which, about two hundred yards south of the entrance gate, is surrounded by a brick wall, bordered with shrubs

> and flowers — some old, some new, but representing
> the love and tender care of those who rest in peace on
> the side of the Green Mountain."

The most interesting point about the American Enniscorthy is its intimate association with the American Independence movement of the 1775 period. "The Virginia Enniscorthy was one of the great centres of the American Revolutionary War," one writer says. Many of the celebrated figures of the War of Independence were frequent visitors there, illustrious leaders like Monroe and Madison, Patrick Henry and Thomas Jefferson.

John Coles was particularly friendly with Jefferson, who later became the third President of the United States. It was Jefferson who wrote the Declaration of American Independence. He designed his own famous residence at Monticello, and devised the decimal system of American coinage. At the time of Tarleton's raid on Monticello, he sent his family for refuge to Enniscorthy.

In the closing stages of the War of Independence it was near Enniscorthy that Lafayette outflanked Cornwallis and forced him to surrender at Yorktown in 1781.

A point of further interest here is the fact that two officers to be captured with Cornwallis at Yorktown were Lake and Needham, whose names are all too well remembered in County Wexford for their part in the Rising of 1798. Lake was in command of the British Forces at the Battle of Vinegar Hill, and Needham was one of the eight general officers under him. Let it be added that the prowess of these two officers in the American encounters of 1781 was far less evident than their gallantry against a defenceless Wexford population seventeen years later.

Cornwallis succeeded Lord Camden as Lord Lieutenant of Ireland in 1798. He arrived in Dublin to take up office on June 20, the eve of the Battle of Vinegar Hill. Having received the reports of the Wexford battles, he wrote to Portland on June 28 — "It shall be one of my first objects to soften the ferocity of our troops, which I am afraid is not confined to the private soldiers" — a condemnation which surely must have included his co-mates of the American war, Lake and Needham. Fr Kavanagh, OSF, the historian of 1798, sums up the character of Lake:

> "Lake was a second Cromwell in his relentless cruelty towards the vanquished, but without a spark of the military genius of that renowned regicide."

It is a source of pride for us that this second Enniscorthy was so closely linked with the American War of Independence, with the birth of the great Republic of the West, true to the magnificent traditions of the parent town, which is honoured everywhere by men of Irish birth for its steadfast loyalty to the cause of Ireland at every crisis of our country's history.

ೞ